Catholic Study Guides for Mary Fabyan Windeatt's

*Saint Margaret Mary and the
Promises of the Sacred Heart of Jesus*

*Saint Francis Solano, Wonder-Worker of the
New World and Apostle of Argentina and Peru*

*Pauline Jaricot, Foundress of the Living Rosary
and the Society for the Propagation of the Faith*

*Saint Paul the Apostle,
The Story of the Apostle to the Gentiles*

RACE for Heaven's Grade 8 Study Guides

Janet P. McKenzie

Biblio Resource Publications, Inc.
Bessemer, Michigan

Saint Margaret Mary Study Guide © 2003 by Janet P. McKenzie
Saint Francis Solano Study Guide © 2004 by Janet P. McKenzie
Pauline Jaricot Study Guide © 2003 by Janet P. McKenzie
Saint Paul the Apostle Study Guide © 2004 by Janet P. McKenzie

Catholic Study Guides for Mary Fabyan Windeatt's Saints Grade 8 © 2007 by Janet P. McKenzie

ISBN 978-1-934185-10-0
Second printing 2015

Published by Biblio Resource Publications, Inc.
108 ½ South Moore Street
Bessemer, MI 49911
info@BiblioResource.com
www.BiblioResource.com

A **R**ead **A**loud **C**urriculum **E**nrichment Product
www.RACEforHeaven.com

All right reserved. With the exception of short excerpts for critical reviews, no part of this work may be reproduced or transmitted in any form or by any means whatsoever without the written permission of the publisher.

Cover photo of Obelisk and Basilica in St. Peters Square, Rome © iofoto - Fotolia.com

Special thanks to Julia Fogassy from Our Father's House for her editorial assistance

Scripture texts in this work are taken from the New American Bible, revised edition © 2010, 1991, 1986, 1970 Confraternity of Christian Doctrine, Washington, D.C. and are used by permission of the copyright owner. All Rights Reserved. No part of the New American Bible may be reproduced in any form without permission in writing from the copyright owner.

All quotations from the Windeatt biographies are excerpted from the edition published by Tan Books and Publisher, Inc. If using the original hardback version of these books, note that the text will be the same but the page numbers will vary from the Tan edition.

Printed in the United States of America

Table of Contents

Spiritual Read Aloud ....i-iv
How to Use These Study Guides ....v-vii

Saint Margaret Mary 1-24
    Poetic Summary of the Life of St. Margaret Mary   1
    Timeline of Events Surrounding the Life of St. Margaret Mary   2
    Map of St. Margaret Mary's France   3
    Catholic Enrichment Activities for Chapters 1 through 41   5-16
    Book Summary Test for *Saint Margaret Mary*   17-18
    Answer Key for Comprehension Questions and Book Summary Test   19-23
    Prayers to the Sacred Heart of Jesus   24

Saint Francis Solano 25-53
    Poetic Summary of the Life of St. Francis Solano   25
    Timeline of Events Surrounding the Life of St. Francis Solano   26
    Map of the World of St. Francis Solano   27
    Map of St. Francis Solano's South America   28
    Catholic Enrichment Activities for Chapters 1 through 18   29-46
    Book Summary Test for *Saint Francis Solano*   47-48
    Answer Key for Comprehension Questions and Book Summary Test   49-53

Pauline Jaricot 55-88
    Poetic Summary of the Life of Pauline Jaricot   55
    Timeline of Events Surrounding the Life of Pauline Jaricot   56
    Map of Pauline Jaricot's France   57
    Catholic Enrichment Activities for Chapters 1 through 41   59-78
    Book Summary Test for *Pauline Jaricot*   79-80
    Answer Key for Comprehension Questions and Book Summary Test   781-88

Saint Paul the Apostle 89-131
    Poetic Summary of the Life of St. Paul   89
    Timeline of Events Surrounding the Life of St. Paul   90
    Map of the World of St. Paul   91
    Catholic Enrichment Activities for Chapters 1 through 43   93-114
    Book Summary Test for *Saint Paul*   115-116
    Answer Key for Comprehension Questions and Book Summary Test   117-127
    A Brief Overview of the New Testament   128
    Roman Citizenship   129-130
    Quotations from the Letters of St. Paul   130-131

Other RACE for Heaven Products... 133-138

Spiritual Read Aloud

Spiritual Reading

In *My Daily Bread, A Summary of the Spiritual Life* by Father Anthony Paone, S.J., Christ tells us,

> My Child, reading and reflecting are a great help to your spiritual life. My doctrine is explained in many books. . . . Some of these books are written simply, and some are very profound and learned. Choose those which will help you most toward a greater understanding and appreciation of My Truth. Do not read to impress others but rather to be impressed yourself. Read so that you may learn My way of thinking and of doing things.

In her book, *Saint Dominic, Preacher of the Rosary and Founder of the Dominican Order*, Mary Fabyan Windeatt quotes St. Dominic as saying, "A little good reading, much prayer and meditation . . . and God will do the rest." Father Peter-Thomas Rohrbach, O.C.D., states that spiritual reading is the "third essential asset for mediation" (after detachment and recollection). The great value he places on the habit of spiritual reading is expressed in his book *Conversation with Christ, An Introduction to Mental Prayer*:

> We live in a world devoid, in great part, of a Christian spirit, in an atmosphere and culture estranged from God. Living in such a non-theological environment makes it difficult for us to remain in contact with the person of Christ and the true purpose of life itself. We must, if we are to remain realistically attached to Christ, combat this atmosphere and surround ourselves with a new one. Constant spiritual reading fills our minds with Christ and His doctrine—it creates this new climate for us.
>
> In former ages, spiritual reading was not as essential for one's prayer life. People lived in a Christian world and culture which was reflected in their laws, customs, amusements, and their very outlook on life. This situation has radically altered in the last two hundred years, and men must now compensate for this deficit through other media, principally reading. And as the de-Christianization of our world continues, the necessity for spiritual reading simultaneously increases. We stand in need of something to bridge the gap between our pagan surroundings and our conversation with Christ—spiritual reading fills this need.
>
> There is today in our country an alarming decline in general reading of all types. It has been estimated that in 1955 an astonishing forty-eight percent of the American adult population reads *no books at all*, and only eighteen percent read from one to four books. The decline in reading is naturally reflected in religious reading as well. And, while the lack of secular reading will occasion a decrease in culture life, the decline in religious reading

will have repercussions of a more serious nature—severe detriment to one's spiritual life. Any serious attempt to better one's life spiritually should, therefore, include the resolution to engage in more spiritual reading.

If we confine our reading to non-Catholic books, magazines and newspapers, we almost automatically exclude ourselves from full development in our prayer life. The maxims and philosophy of life expressed in these avenues of communication slowly begin to seep into our lives until eventually they occupy a ruling position. We will not have surrounded ourselves with a new climate; rather, the non-Catholic climate will have engulfed us.

As this decry of the "de-Christianization of our world" was written in 1956, one can safely surmise that the necessity of cultivating the habit of spiritual reading can only have grown in the past several decades.

Spiritual Read Aloud

As supported above, spiritual reading is an essential element of every Christian's life. However, as demonstrated by the ancient practice within monasteries of spiritual read-aloud, this habit is a powerful tool for shared community growth in the spiritual life. For Catholic families, the practice of reading spiritual books aloud produces four desirable effects:

I. It reinforces the habit of spiritual reading for each member of the family and allows each member to practice this habit regardless of age.
II. It reinforces the habit of spiritual conversation if the reading results in even a general discussion of the values and virtues being portrayed in the story.
III. It strengthens the family as the domestic Church where members exist to learn and live the Faith together for the support and enrichment of all family members.
IV. It allows the discussion and demonstration of the practical application of the Faith for all age levels.

The Habit of Spiritual Reading

As outlined above, establishing the habit of daily spiritual reading is essential to our spiritual growth. Through read-aloud, children can be taught at an early age that daily spiritual reading is a fun, rewarding exercise. Do make this time together pleasant by allowing the children to do crafts, draw, play quietly with puzzles, toys, etc. As long as their attention is not divided and they can participate in a discussion of the reading afterwards, allow quiet activity. One cannot expect children to sit piously with hands clasped prayerfully throughout the read-aloud session! As the children get older, encourage them to read other spiritual books, including the Bible, during a quiet time of their own. Model this habit by allowing them to observe your habit of daily spiritual reading as well. Although the family read-aloud sessions may be as long as thirty minutes, private spiritual reading times may be considerably shorter depending on the habits and temperament of each child.

The Habit of Spiritual Conversation

This habit, for many families, may begin with spiritual read-aloud. When each member of the family participates in a spiritual discussion of a religious book, the practice of discussing matters of faith and Christ-like living begins to form. If the formation of holy habits and imitation of the saints is the goal, these discussions will become commonplace in the home as each member checks the others on their actions and words. As family members become more comfortable and open about spiritual matters, this practice will soon spread into other areas of their lives. Spiritual discussions with friends and other relatives will become more natural and in fact become important topics to be discussed. Sharing one's own spirituality and encouraging others to become more open about matters of faith will then become an integral pattern of living.

Strengthening the Domestic Church

As we read more about the saints and their lives and begin to share our faith more openly with others, we realize the importance of holy companionship—living with others who share our faith ideas and supporting each other in our attempts to become more like Christ. Families begin to grow together in their knowledge of the Catholic faith and become more willing to support each other throughout the ups and downs of community living. We begin to "bear one another's burdens with peace and harmony and unselfishness." Just as Christ has His Church to help bring salvation to all, we—as family members—have each other to provide mutual support and encouragement in our efforts to enter the narrow gate. Within our families, we can create the Catholic culture that is missing from our world's culture.

The Practical Application of the Faith for All Age Levels

When lives of the saints are read aloud in the family setting, all aged children can participate in a discussion of the imitation of the saint's virtues and holy habits. Each member can help others understand how to apply the lessons the saints teach us on a practical level. All family members can help choose a particular habit or virtue upon which to focus. A reward system can be established for virtuous behavior. A family "plan of attack" on non-virtuous habits and attitudes can be developed, implemented, checked, and revised. All members can be encouraged and taught to imitate Christ by the imitation of His saints.

Summary

Regular family read-loud sessions that center around the lives of the saints will benefit the family with an increased interest in reading—especially saintly literature, a growth in vocabulary, and an improved sense of family unity. Additionally, family members will be encouraged to develop the habit of spiritual reading on their own, will become more comfortable and experienced with spiritual conversation, and be able to apply the Truths of the Catholic faith, on a practical level, to all aspects of their lives—no matter what their age. The customs, habits, and attitudes of the family will more and more reflect those of the Catholic culture. Perseverance in this simple daily ritual will help to "bridge the gap between our pagan surroundings and our conversation with Christ."

When Mother Reads Aloud

When Mother reads aloud the past
Seems real as every day;
I hear the tramp of armies vast,
I see the spears and lances cast,
I join the thrilling fray;
Brave knights and ladies fair and proud
I meet when Mother reads aloud.

When Mother reads aloud, far lands
Seem very near and true;
I cross the desert's gleaming sands,
Or hunt the jungle's prowling bands,
Or sail the ocean blue;
Far heights, whose peaks the cold mists
  shroud,
I scale, when Mother reads aloud.

When Mother reads aloud I long
For noble deeds to do—
To help the right, redress the wrong,
It seems so easy to be strong, so simple
  to be true,
O, thick and fast the visions crowd
When Mother reads aloud.
  –Anonymous

The Reading Mother

I had a mother who read to me
Sagas of pirates who scoured the sea,
Cutlasses clenched in their yellow teeth,
"Blackbirds" stowed in the hold beneath.

I had a mother who read me plays
Of ancient and gallant and golden days
Stories of Marmion and Ivanhoe,
Which every boy has a right to know.

I had a mother who read me tales
Of Gelert, the hound of the hills of
  Wales,
True to his trust till his tragic death,
Faithfulness blest with his final breath.

I had a mother who read me things
That wholesome life to the boy-heart
  brings—
Stories that stir with an upward touch,
O, that each mother of boys were such.

You may have tangible wealth untold,
Caskets of jewels and coffers of gold.
Richer than I you can never be—
I had a mother who read to me.
  –Strickland Gullilan

How to Use These Study Guides

✸REVIEW✸ Vocabulary

Vocabulary words are listed at the beginning of each lesson. Words on the left are secular words and are given within the sentence structure. Allow students to guess the meaning of the italicized word before looking it up. This helps them to surmise the meaning from context, a skill that enhances reading comprehension and strengthens vocabulary. Vocabulary words listed in the right-hand column are Catholic vocabulary words. Help students identify any suffixes, prefixes or root words that might give clues to the word's meaning. To help with definitions and proper usage, use a dictionary. For Catholic vocabulary words, use a Catholic encyclopedia, dictionary, or catechism.

❓❓❓ Comprehension Questions/Narration Prompts

These questions are appropriate for all age levels. They can be used several ways, depending on a student's ability. For students with difficulty in reading comprehension, read and briefly discuss these questions before reading the chapter. Discuss, too, the sub-title provided under each chapter heading in the study guide. The student will then know what content to watch for within the reading. If read afterward, the questions become a *test of,* rather than an *aid to,* comprehension. For students with adequate comprehension skills, use the questions for oral review after the reading to insure that important content has been absorbed.

Use these questions too as prompts for narration, which is simply the oral retelling of the story in the student's own words. It is a helpful tool to determine the level of each student's comprehension. All ages may benefit from the practice of narration. If done within a mixed age group, begin with the youngest students and have the older students add details to the already-related story.

Answers to comprehension questions are provided in the answer key.

Forming Opinions/Drawing Conclusions

More than relating events, these questions require the student to develop an opinion, or to uncover or discover material not expressly stated in the text. They are designed to develop thinking skills and do not usually require the use of any outside resources. Use this section with children grades five and up as the basis for discussion or as a writing assignment.

For Further Study

Appropriate for upper elementary through high school grades, this section requires the use of additional reference materials. These activities invite students to look more deeply at the historical events and people that shaped the times of each character. Topics in this section may be used for honing research skills, or for oral presentations and/or written reports.

Growing in Holiness

These activities are different from the others in that they do not involve discussion or study as much as personal action and interior reflection. They can perhaps be considered "conversion activities" or "life lessons." By applying the spiritual lessons of the story to everyday life, the student is encouraged to develop habits in imitation of the saints—which is an imitation of Christ Himself. Remember to reinforce these activities with the student and to comment when they are observed in action.

 Geography

The map provided with this study guide serves to orient the students with respect to space—*where* the action of the story is taking place—as well as to acquaint them with common geographical landmarks. Permission is hereby granted to photocopy maps for family or classroom use.

 Timeline Work

The creation of a timeline allows students to place the story's events within a wider historical framework. Simple directions for making a timeline are included in the study guide. Students will need plain paper, colored markers, and a ruler.

✓ **Checking the Catechism**

For older students, these activities require a copy of the *Catechism of the Catholic Church* (*CCC*) or its *Compendium*. The references for the more concise *Compendium* appear in parentheses after the *CCC* citations. Older students can read aloud—and then discuss—the stated text paragraphs with an adult.

For younger students, use any grade-appropriate catechism to review the doctrines and terms as specified. An excellent activity book for multi-grades is Ignatius Press' *100 Activities Based on the Catechism of the Catholic Church* by Ellen Rossini. Discuss together how the specific topics from the catechism are illustrated in the thoughts and actions of the characters in the book.

📖 **Searching Scripture**

Familiarize the student with the inspired Word of God by studying the biblical passages provided. Strengthen these exercises by occasionally requiring memorization of the verse(s). Stress that knowledge of Scripture is an important part of our faith education.

Note that Ms. Windeatt used the Douay-Rheims translation of the Bible, which was the translation in use in the United States until 1970 when it was replaced by the New American Bible in the *Lectionary of Mass*. The Douay-Rheims translation is taken from the Latin Vulgate, whereas the New American translation comes from the original languages of Hebrew, Aramaic or Greek (as the case may be for each specific book). For this reason, some of the books' names (as well as some of the Psalms' numbers) differ between these two translations. When these differences occur in the biblical citations within this study guide, the New American references are given first with the Douay-Rheims references following in parentheses. All biblical references used in this study guide are from the New American translation.

 **Test**

The purpose of the test is to ensure that the student has comprehended the important events in each saint's life as well as the lessons the story intends to impart. An answer key is provided for these questions.

In addition to the test, many students will benefit from the completion of a book report. See RACE for Heaven's *Alternative Book Reports for Catholic Students* for additional information on book reports specifically geared toward saint biographies. Consider requiring each student to choose one of these reports or activities upon completion of the Windeatt biography.

Warning

These study guides are comprehensive. They contain activities for a variety of age levels and areas of study. Do **not** attempt to complete every activity for every lesson. Do only those exercises that are suitable for the needs of your current situation. Resist the impulse to be so thorough that the story line of the book is lost, and the read-aloud sessions become dreaded rather than anticipated. The activities are designed to enhance your reading—not to become the dictating tyrant of your read-aloud time together. If you are using these guides for young audiences, consider just using the comprehension and opinion questions as well as the "Growing in Holiness" section; use the maps as a geographical visual aid. Re-read the books to complete the more advanced activities in later years.

Another suggestion is to use the activities designed for older students in coordination with their history, geography, writing and/or religious curriculum. Each study guide could also be used as a complete unit study for hectic times when regular school may not be in session such as Advent, times of family stress (the birth of a new sibling, for example) or over the summer months. In reading the book and completing the activities, subjects such as religion, reading, writing, geography, and history can all be easily covered.

The most important rules to the successful use of these enrichment activities are
1. Be creative rather than obsessive.
2. Be flexible rather than overly structured.
3. Enjoy!

Study Guide for

*Saint Margaret Mary
and the Promises of the
Sacred Heart of Jesus*

St. Margaret Mary

Margaret Alacoque was sick as a child.
She lived with her aunts who were easily riled.
She prayed for a cure,
And Mary said "Sure";
Her vow to be a sister was duly filed.

Margaret's brothers came back—home to stay.
Her aunts and her uncle then moved away.
Happiness returned,
Though her vocation spurned.
A priest intervened, and her brothers did sway.

The Visitation Order is where Margaret went.
Because she was different, she caused much dissent.
Her visions from God,
Her prayer life was odd—
Her peers started to question her mind and intent.

God sent her a priest-friend to counsel and guide her.
With her superior he verified her.
The visions were real;
He did reveal.
But not many sisters would stand beside her.

Jesus told her about His Sacred Heart—
How many sins hurt it. Could she do her part
To make up for sin
By suffering within?
His mercy and love to others impart.

First Fridays remember to commune with our Lord.
Each week make a Holy Hour, His Heart be adored!
His Heart shall be known.
His mercy be shown.
By our reparation, His graces outpoured!

Think what you can learn from this saint and her tale.
How you can apply it to help you prevail.
Then mold what you do
And boldly pursue
Her pattern of holiness. Follow her trail.

Timeline of Events

Year	Event
1617	Death of St. Rose of Lima; death of Pocahontas
1619	First African slaves brought to North America
1639	Death of St. Martin de Porres; first printing press in North America
1640	Heresy of Jansensim spread throughout France (until around 1800)
1641	Birth of Claude de la Colombière on February 2nd; founding of Quakers
1642	Birth of Isaac Newton; death of Galileo Galilei; martyrdom of St. Isaac Jogues
1645	Death of St. John Masias; Capuchin monks explore the Congo River
1647	Birth of Margaret Alacoque on July 22nd; invention of the bayonet in France
1648	Peace of Westphalia ends the Thirty Years' War; mirrors manufactured in Italy
1650	Tea first drunk in England; Charles Stuart lands in Scotland, proclaimed Charles II
1658	Death of Oliver Cromwell; John Milton begins writing Paradise Lost
1660	Establishment of English monarchy; death of St. Louise de Marillac
1665	Canonization of St. Francis de Sales; Great Plague of London
1671	Margaret Mary enters the Visitation convent at Paray-le-Monial on June 20th
1673	First great revelation of the Sacred Heart – December 27th; Father Marquette and Louis Joliet sail down the Mississippi River; Father Hennipin discovers Niagara Falls
1674	Second and third revelations of the Sacred Heart; invention of the tourniquet
1675	Father Claude de la Colombière arrives in Paray-le-Monial; last great revelation of the Sacred Heart; Father and Margaret Mary consecrate themselves to the Sacred Heart; composer Antonio Vivaldi born; invention of differential calculus
1676	Father de la Colombière goes to London; death of Pope Clement X
1678	Titus Oates pretends there is a "Popish plot" to murder Charles II; Father de la Colombière imprisoned in London – November 24; freed December 21st
1679	Act of Habeas Corpus passes in England forbidding imprisonment without trial
1680	Clocks now have minute hand; Dodo bird becomes extinct; death of Kateri Tekakwitha; penny post (letters carried for one penny) established in London
1681	Father de la Colombière returns to Paray-le-Monial; first checks used in England
1682	Death of Father de la Colombière at Paray-le-Monial, France in February
1685	Margaret Mary made Mistress of Novices for a period of two years in January; death of Charles II of England; birth of composers J.S. Bach and George Handel
1687	England's James II issues the Declaration of Indulgence giving freedom of worship
1688	Twelfth and final promise of Sacred Heart made to Margaret Mary in May; dedication of the Sacred Heart chapel at Paray-le-Monial on September 7th
1689	Peter the Great becomes Tsar of Russia; English Parliament passes Bill of Rights
1690	Death of Margaret Mary Alacoque on October 17th; founding of city of Calcutta
1694	Birth of St. Paul of the Cross, Passionists' founder; birth of French writer Voltaire
1715	Death of France's King Louis XIV (54-year reign); Jacobite rebellion in Scotland
1824	Margaret Mary declared venerable (beatified in 1864; canonized in 1920; Father de la Colombière canonized in 1992); John Quincy Adams elected President
1856	Feast of the Sacred Heart extended to the Universal Church as a solemnity to be celebrated on the Friday after the second Sunday after Pentecost; James Buchanan elected President of the United States; Woodrow Wilson born

Saint Margaret Mary

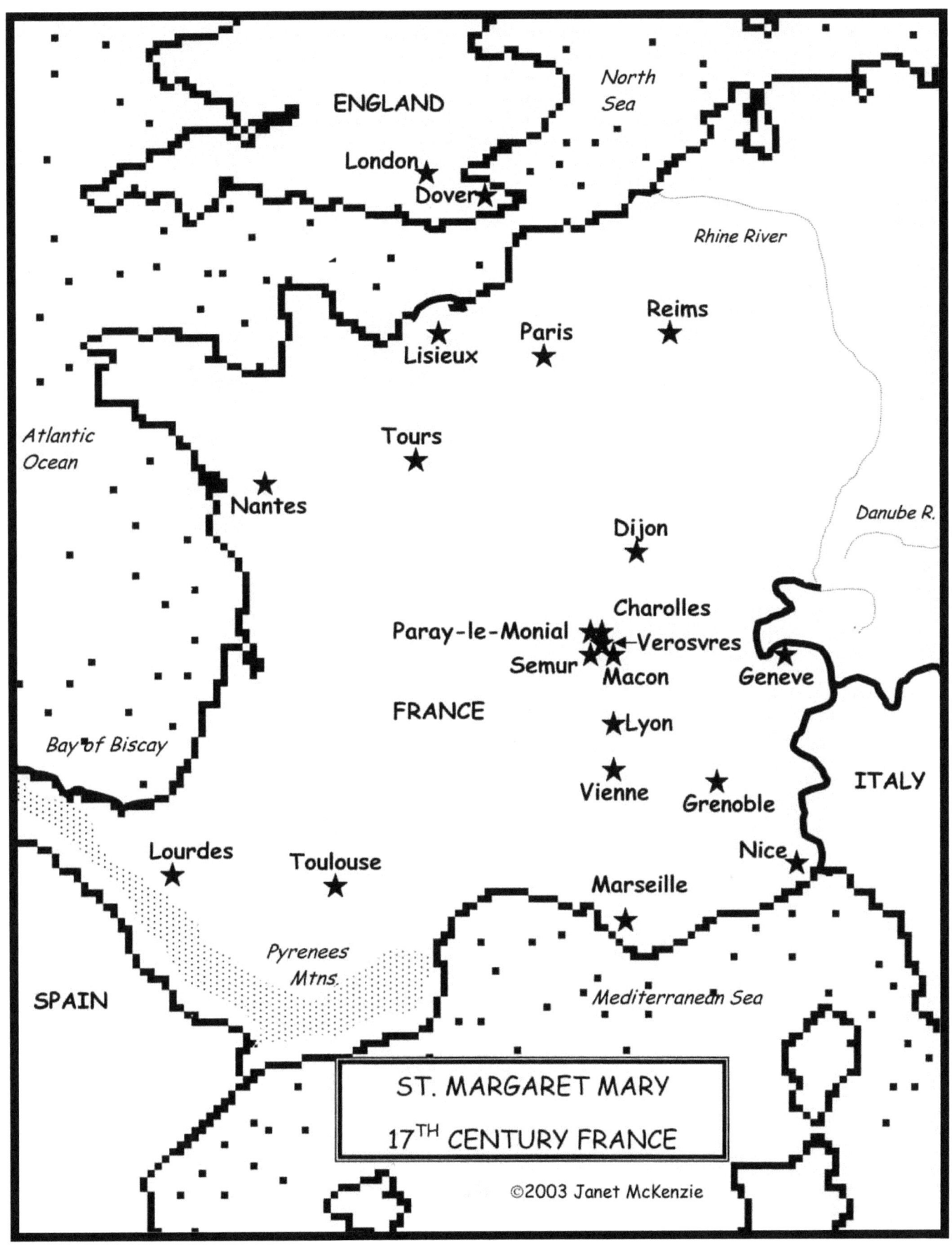

Chapters 1 through 4—In Which Margaret and Her Mother Suffer Illness and Misfortune

 Vocabulary

put in a second *querulous* voice
said Benedicta Delaroche *brusquely*
Poor Clares
Ursulines

 Comprehension Questions/Narration Prompts
1. What circumstances caused Margaret and her mother to live on the farm with Margaret's aunts and uncle? How did these relatives treat Margaret?
2. What promise did Margaret make in Chapter 2? What was its result?
3. What are the "New Troubles" of Chapter 3?
4. What bothersome problem worried Margaret?

 Forming Opinions/Drawing Conclusions

Why do you think Margaret felt guilty about dancing and having fun? How can you apply Father Anthony's advice regarding these activities to yourself?

 Growing in Holiness

"The main thing now was to pray for the gift of faith." (page 8) Memorize and pray daily the following Act of Faith: "O my God, I firmly believe that You are the one God in Three Divine Persons, Father, Son, and Holy Spirit; I believe that Your Divine Son became man and died for all sins, and that He will come to judge the living and the dead. I believe these and all truths which the Holy Catholic Church teaches, because You have revealed them, who can neither deceive nor be deceived."

 Timeline Work

Taping sheets of plain paper end-to-end, make a timeline representing the years from 1617 through 1856. Let three inches equal 25 years. Mark on your timeline the dates and events from 1617 through 1665, using information from page 2 of this study guide.

✓ **Checking the Catechism**

Older students may read the following text paragraphs in the *Catechism of the Catholic Church* (*CCC*): 26, 142-44, 150, 1814-16, and 2087-89 (28-32, 386, and 442) on faith. If desired, complete Activity #32 in *100 Activities Based on the Catechism of the Catholic Church* (*100 Activities*). Younger students may study the theological virtues of faith, hope, and love in their catechisms.

 Searching Scripture

Read the following scriptural passages on faith: Matthew 17:19-20, John 6:47, Romans 10:10-11, 1 Corinthians 16:13, 2 Corinthians 5:7, Galatians 5:6, Ephesians 2:8, and Hebrews 11:1 and 11:6.

Chapters 5 through 8—In Which Margaret's Vocation and Mission Begin to Be Understood

 Vocabulary

looking at him in *abject* misery
unable to *muster* more

Confirmation
Order of the Visitation of Mary

 Comprehension Questions/Narration Prompts
1. What sorrows had Margaret's mother endured in the past several years? What additional stress caused her to have a "nervous breakdown"?
2. Why did Margaret want to enter a convent? For what gift did she ask at Confirmation?
3. In what way did the Franciscan friar who conducted a mission in Margaret's parish help her?
4. Why did Margaret not want to go to the Ursuline convent in Macon?

 Forming Opinions/Drawing Conclusions
1. "In fact, perhaps you can become a greater saint here at home than you could ever hope to be by living in the cloister." (page 27) How can holiness be obtained by living in the world? Compare this with the opportunities for holiness as a religious.
2. "Selfishness is always wrong." (page 31) What commandments can selfishness break?
3. Chrysostom tries to discern Margaret's vocation for her. Why is this difficult and risky?

 Growing in Holiness
Margaret's "mission" is discussed several times. The friar explains that children do not belong to their parents but are only lent to them by God "until they're ready to begin the work He placed them on earth to do" (page 31). Begin to discern what work God may have for you to accomplish. Why did He uniquely create you at this specific time?

 Geography
Trace the map on page 3 of this study guide. Color these seas, oceans, and rivers blue: Atlantic, North, Mediterranean, Bay of Biscay, Rhine, and Danube. Color the Pyrenees Mountains brown. (The map will be completed in the lesson for Chapters 32-34.)

✓ **Checking the Catechism**
Older students may read text paragraphs 1285, 1293-96, and 1300-1321 in the *CCC* (250, and 265-270). If desired, complete Activity #88 in *100 Activities*. Younger students may review the Sacrament of Confirmation in their catechisms.

 Searching Scripture
Read 2 Corinthians 1:21-22, Ephesians 1:13 and 4:30, and Revelation (Apocalypse) 9:4 on God's seal as well as Matthew 3:13-17, and Acts 2:1-4 and 8:14-17 on the Holy Spirit.

Chapters 9 through 12—In Which Sister Margaret Mary Encounters Difficulties in the Convent

---

 Vocabulary

Margaret Mary's feeling of *loathing*　　　*choir sister*
Margaret Mary was *aghast*　　　*private revelation*

 Comprehension Questions/Narration Prompts

1. What is Mother Thouvant's explanation of meditation? What is the point of the reading?
2. What is the summary of the vocation of a Visitation nun given in Chapter 10?
3. What difficulties did Sister Margaret Mary encounter in the convent?
4. What persuaded Mother de Saumaise that Sister Margaret Mary should be allowed to make her Profession as a Visitation nun? When did this take place?
5. What did the Visitation superior request of Sister Margaret Mary in order to resolve the "so-called visions" (page 57) that she reported?

 Forming Opinions/Drawing Conclusions

1. Why was it important that Sister Margaret Mary observe the Rule's regulations regarding meditation time, ways of prayer, and obedience?
2. What reasons can you give to explain why Sister Margaret Mary would emphasize God's love when she most often visualized Him as He appeared on the road to Calvary?
3. Putting yourself in the place of Mother de Saumaise, why do you think it was so difficult to believe that Sister Margaret Mary was experiencing great graces?

 Growing in Holiness

Jesus rewarded Sister Margaret Mary's obedience in eating the loathsome cheese with great graces and favors. Think of a food, activity, or person that is "loathsome" to you and begin to practice mortification by consuming that food, participating in that activity, or spending cheerful time with that person. Imitate St. Margaret Mary by overcoming yourself!

✓ **Checking the Catechism**

Sister Margaret Mary often visualized Jesus on His way to Calvary. He is, however, more than our Savior. If desired, complete Activity #44 in *100 Activities*. Younger students may reference their catechisms to discover other names used to refer to Jesus. (Remember that praying the name of Jesus is the simplest prayer.) Older students may read text paragraph 67 in the *CCC* (10) regarding private revelation.

 Searching Scripture

Read Isaiah (Isaias) 50:6 and 53:3-9 on the image of the suffering servant, a prophecy perfectly fulfilled in Jesus. Read too the Christological hymn of Philippians 2:6-11. Does a crucifix adequately portray how He much suffered for us?

Chapters 13 through 16—In Which Sister Margaret Mary Continues to Be Misunderstood

⭐REVIEW⭐ Vocabulary
hastened to *allay* such fears
it was wonderfully *edifying*

octave
approbation

 Comprehension Questions/Narration Prompts
1. What happened on December 27, 1673? What did our Lord say to Margaret Mary?
2. What opinion of Sr. Margaret Mary did the two priests express to Mother de Saumaise? What was their suggested remedy? How did our Lord console Margaret Mary?
3. What did Christ ask of Margaret Mary during the octave of Corpus Christi in 1674?
4. How did the other sisters react to Sister Margaret Mary and her visions?

 Forming Opinions/Drawing Conclusions
1. Mother de Saumaise stressed the importance of the Holy Rule when she asked what would happen "if each one here decided to take upon herself this or that extra devotion?" (page 73). Discuss the value of rules in living together as a peaceful family.
2. What virtues did Sister Margaret Mary display in her trials? Write down three specific changes you can make to your own behavior or attitude that would imitate these virtues.
3. Why do you suppose that our Lord chose this particular time and place to make known the yearning of His Heart for the love of souls?

 Growing in Holiness
Sister Margaret Mary complained to her superior that many of the sisters were not faithful to the Rule of the community; they gave in or made excuses "when they're tired or out-of-sorts" (page 62). Additionally, they were inclined to pride and often preferred their own will. Assess yourself on these points. Do you disobey the rule of your family or parents? Do you make excuses and get "out of sorts"? Are you inclined to pride? Do you prefer your own will to that of God or other superiors? Check yourself daily on these virtues.

✓ **Checking the Catechism**
Sister Margaret Mary is accused of presumption and sacrilege. Read about these two sins in text paragraphs 2091-92 and 2732, and 2120 of the *CCC* (442 and 445) or your own catechism.

 Searching Scripture
Read Matthew 13:57. Although we know that God gives special graces to many people, why is it so difficult to believe that those we know and see every day may be one of these chosen souls? Are you yourself open each moment to God's graces and His special plan for you? Read Jeremiah (Jeremias) 29: 11. God has a special plan for each of our lives.

Chapters 17 through 19—In Which Sister Margaret Mary Continues to Upset the Community, and a New Confessor Arrives

 Vocabulary

exclaimed the infirmarian *incredulously* *Holy Hour*
accord you my protection *Holy Water*

 Comprehension Questions/Narration Prompts
1. Under what condition did Mother de Saumaise allow Sister Margaret Mary to make her Holy Hour and receive Holy Communion on the First Fridays?
2. What was the miracle that Mother de Saumaise felt happened at the Visitation convent?
3. What three practices of Sister Margaret Mary upset the other sisters?
4. What was Father de la Colombière's first impression of Sister Margaret Mary?

 Forming Opinions/Drawing Conclusions
1. Of the three groups mentioned on page 88, decide honestly where your sentiments would be in similar circumstances—believing Sister Margaret Mary, not believing but feeling her to be harmless, or frantic with fear that she is possessed by the devil. Consider how often we are critical and judgmental of others.
2. What do you think Mother de Saumaise's reaction will be to Father de la Colombière's remark that Sister Margaret Mary is a "chosen soul"?

 For Further Study
Research the life of St. Claude de la Colombière, a Jesuit priest declared venerable in 1880 and canonized in 1992, who did much to promote devotion to the Sacred Heart of Jesus.

 Growing in Holiness
Father de la Colombière stated that he would hear confessions during Ember Days, days that observe the four seasons. Fasting and partial abstinence have been the custom in Catholic homes on these days until recent years. Renew this custom in your family by observing Ember Days as days of prayer for vocations to the priesthood and religious life.

 Timeline Work
Add the dates and events from 1671 through 1680 to your timeline.

Searching Scripture
Consider the heavy burden of responsibility that rested on Mother de Saumaise as she made decisions regarding Sister Margaret Mary and the entire Visitation community. Read Luke 12:48b and Hebrews 13:17 regarding accountability.

Chapters 20 through 22—In Which Sister Margaret Mary Finds and Loses a Faithful Friend

 Vocabulary

joy *inexplicably* drained out
that poor *deluded* soul

Church of England
Garden of Olives

 Comprehension Questions/Narration Prompts
1. Why was Sister Margaret Mary at first unable to confide in Father de la Colombière?
2. What does "reparation" mean and for what does our Lord want reparation?
3. What happened on June 16, 1675, at the Visitation convent in Paray-le-Monial, France?
4. What two ideas of the Sacred Heart devotion seemed strange to Catholics at this time?
5. Where was Father de la Colombière sent in the fall of 1676 and why?

 Forming Opinions/Drawing Conclusions
1. Explain what Sister Margaret Mary means when she calls the Lord and the members of His Church "one big family" (page 98). How do the terms "Mystical Body of Christ" and "Communion of Saints" enhance this explanation?
2. What feelings might Father de la Colombière have as he prepares to leave for a foreign country that is currently persecuting members of the Catholic Church?

 For Further Study

Research the history of devotion to the Sacred Heart including those men and women mentioned on page 97. Prepare a short report or oral presentation to be given to your family. What religious climate in France at this time made opportune the promotion of God's mercy?

 Growing in Holiness

Begin to make a weekly Holy Hour of Reparation in honor of our Lord's request to St. Margaret Mary. If you are unable to go before the Blessed Sacrament for this hour, conduct a Holy Hour at home in front of a crucifix. Sing hymns of praise, pray the rosary, read biblical passages, and spend time quietly with the Lord. Offer acts of reparation throughout the week. Speak to others about the love and mercy abounding in the Sacred Heart of Jesus.

✓ **Checking the Catechism**

Read about God's attributes in your catechism. Older students may read text paragraphs 211, 270, 545, 1846-48, 1864, and 2840 in the *CCC* (107, 391, and 595) on God's mercy.

 Searching Scripture

Read Psalm 136 (135) which lists the merciful acts of God in creation, toward the Isrealites, and toward us. Read too Matthew 5:7, Luke 15:11-24, and Ephesians 2:4.

Chapters 23 through 25—In Which Our Lord Makes Promises, Letters Arrive from Father de la Colombière, and Sister Margaret Mary Becomes a Victim Soul

Vocabulary
legions of angels
all the *bigotry* and persecution
Protestants
victim

Comprehension Questions/Narration Prompts
1. What does Mother de Saumaise state is the "all-powerful key that opens Heaven"?
2. How did Sister Margaret Mary look upon those who misunderstood and persecuted her?
3. Name some of the trials of the Duchess of York, Mary Beatrice d'Este.
4. What is the "extremely difficult command" of Chapter 25?

Forming Opinions/Drawing Conclusions
1. Explain in your own words the first eight promises of the Sacred Heart of Jesus.
2. "There's always an Easter after Good Friday" (page 114). What does this mean?

For Further Study
Begin to research the political climate of seventeenth-century England by studying the following characters: King Charles II; Queen Catherine Braganza; William of Orange; the Duchess of York, Mary Beatrice d'Este; and Pope Clement X.

Growing in Holiness
"... hadn't Our Lord Himself set the example for patience in suffering ... when His enemies had scorned and laughed at His teachings, He had maintained a charitable silence" (page 114). Consider this practice of "charitable silence" when teased or unjustly accused.

Checking the Catechism
"Oh, what a miserable thing pride is! It's the root of all the sin ..." (page 124). Older students can read about pride in the *CCC* in text paragraphs 1784, 1866, 2094, 2317, 2540, and 2728 (398 and 442), while younger students review pride and sin in their catechisms.

Searching Scripture
Research three passages of text that refer to scripture: "such childlike faith and trust in Divine Providence," Psalm 131 (130); "They were taking the easy path to Hell instead of the difficult path to Heaven," Matthew 7:13-14; and "My God, have pity on me according to the greatness of Thy mercy!," Psalm 51 (50):3-4. Read these scriptures pertaining to pride: Proverbs 11:2, Proverbs 16:18, Sirach (Ecclesiasticus) 10:12-17, and Matthew 23:12.; and silence: Psalm 141 (140):3.

Chapters 26 through 28—In Which Sister Margaret Mary Receives a New Superior, and in England Father de la Colombière Gets Arrested

 Vocabulary

efforts . . . had come to *naught*
had gained so many *adherents*
Divine Justice
Popish Plot

 Comprehension Questions/Narration Prompts
1. What did the new superior of the convent order Sister Margaret Mary to do?
2. What were some of the adversities that Father de la Colombière faced in England?
3. Where did Father de la Colombière believe that true strength lies for everyone?
4. Why was Father de la Colombière arrested on November 24, 1678?
5. What did Father de la Colombière request be smuggled into prison for him?

 Forming Opinions/Drawing Conclusions
1. Why is "real progress in the other virtues" difficult without the virtue of obedience?
2. Why do you suppose that the new superior wanted Sister Margaret Mary to be more like the other sisters in the convent? Why do many people find "different" so difficult?

 For Further Study
Continue researching conditions in seventeenth-century England and France by studying Louis XIV of France, Titus Oates of England, Oliver Cromwell, and King Charles I.

 Growing in Holiness
Father de la Colombière was prepared to become a martyr for the Faith, as should we all. But remember that the highest sanctity does not consist of revelations, miracles, and martyrdom, but in pure faith and the unflagging fulfillment of our daily duty. Everything lies in our intention. "A soul that lives in union with God does nothing that is not supernatural, and its commonest actions, instead of separating it from God, on the contrary, draw it nearer to Him." (Blessed Elizabeth of the Trinity) Apply this thought of Blessed Elizabeth's in your obedience to others and your obedience to daily duty.

✓ **Checking the Catechism**
Older students can read about the Sacred Heart of Jesus in the *CCC* in text paragraphs 478 and 2669 (93) while younger students review this topic in their own catechisms.

 Searching Scripture
Read these scripture passages regarding the devotion to the Sacred Heart of Jesus: Exodus 24:7b, Psalm 29 (28):10, Matthew 11:29, and John 19:34.

Saint Margaret Mary

Chapters 29 through 31—In Which Father de la Colombière Returns to France and Comes to the Aid of Sister Margaret Mary

---

 Vocabulary

A storm of jeers and *catcalls* rang
long weeks of *convalescence*

chapter meeting
conscience

 Comprehension Questions/Narration Prompts

1. What were the charges against Father de la Colombière during his court proceeding? Why did the judge hold Father de la Colombière over to trial for his life?
2. When and why was Father de la Colombière released from prison?
3. What did Father de la Colombière accomplish during his stay in England? What important task did he not accomplish?

Forming Opinions/Drawing Conclusions

1. "Mother Greyfié was a most devout religious, but also of an exceedingly practical turn of mind." (pages 159-160) What does this mean? How did it affect Mother Greyfié's governance of the convent at Paray-le-Monial?
2. How did Father de la Colombière know that Sister Margaret Mary was not being deceived by the devil? What made his argument to Mother Greyfié convincing?
3. Father de la Colombière explains that the task of a soul is to abandon itself to God, trusting in Him completely—to accept each cross as a key to our own particular door to Heaven. How can you apply this to your own growth in holiness?
4. Explain, in your own words, Father de la Colombière's explanation of the Devotion to the Sacred Heart as found on pages 164-167.
5. In what ways had sickness been a great grace to Father de la Colombière?

 Growing in Holiness

"Love grows by loving." (page 165) Father de la Colombière describes several steps in growing in love: Be sure your soul is in the state of Sanctifying Grace; increase your understanding of Jesus' love and suffering; offer Him reparation by receiving Him often in Holy Communion, especially on the First Friday of each month; continue to make a Holy Hour each Thursday; and accept the suffering God gives you as suffering is closely related to love. Remember to put your confidence not in yourself but in the Sacred Heart of Jesus. Recite often: "Sacred Heart of Jesus, have mercy on us!"

 Searching Scripture

Find the following quotation from page 149 in the Bible: "Father, forgive them, for they know not what they do." Also read about Jesus' agony in the Garden of Gethesmane in Mark 14:32-42.

Chapters 32 through 34—In Which Father de la Colombière Dies, and More Promises Are Made

---

 Vocabulary

A comfortable carriage was *procured*
they shall never be *effaced* from it
holy obedience
Patroness

Comprehension Questions/Narration Prompts
1. What happened on February 15, 1682? What was the miracle of February 6, 1685?
2. What did Mother Melin request of our Lord so that she might be convinced of Sister Margaret Mary's visions? What was her next request regarding Sister Margaret Mary?
3. Name some of the concerns when Sister Margaret Mary was appointed Novice Mistress.
4. Name the three additional promises of the Sacred Heart as revealed in Chapter 33.
5. What surprise did the novices plan for Mother Margaret Mary for the feast day of her patroness, St. Margaret of Antioch, on July 20th?

 Forming Opinions/Drawing Conclusions
1. Explain the phrase "like a corpse in the hands of the washers of the dead" (page 172).
2. "Stop worrying. Invoke him." (page 172) Explain this and how you can apply it.

 For Further Study

Research the lives of the founders of the Visitation Order, St. Francis de Sales and St. Jane de Chantal. What is the "spirit of the Order" (page 177)?

 Growing in Holiness

Choose a patron saint of your own based upon your name, your birth date, or your baptismal date. Research the life of this saint; then compose a short prayer to be used each day to invoke this saint's aid. Throughout the day, ask your saint to help you by praying, "Saint (name), pray for me. Saint (name), come to my aid!"

 Geography

Complete the map started in the lesson for Chapters 5 through 8 by labeling all cities red and the four countries green. On the map provided, cities are indicated with a star, and countries are in bold capitals.

 Checking the Catechism

Page 181 contains references not only to invoking the power of the saints but also to celebrating their feast days. Older students can read about the saints in the *CCC* in text paragraphs 61, 828, 946-48, 956-62, 1161, 1173, 1195, 1474-77, 2030, 2156, and 2683-84 (165, 240, 242, 294, 429, and 564). If desired, complete Activity #82 in *100 Activities*. Younger students may review the doctrine of the communion of saints in their catechisms.

Chapters 35 through 37—In Which The Other Sisters Begin to Understand Mother Margaret Mary, and She Begins to Teach the Children

 Vocabulary

neglectful treatment *meted* out to Him
occasional *lapses* into sin

refectory
Enthronement of the Sacred Heart

 Comprehension Questions/Narration Prompts
1. What was Mother Melin's plan to get the community to accept our Lord's apparitions regarding the devotion to the Sacred Heart? How well did it work?
2. When is the Feast of the Sacred Heart? Why is it celebrated on that day?
3. What caused the sisters to change their hearts toward Mother Margaret Mary?
4. What new title did Mother Margaret Mary receive in 1687?
5. What is Mother Margaret Mary's definition of a saint? What is her "key to holiness"?

 Forming Opinions/Drawing Conclusions
1. What does the connection between Mother Margaret Mary's reception of Holy Communion on the First Fridays of every month and Sister Frances Rosalie's health teach us about God's desire for reparation? How can you apply this teaching to your life?
2. Mother Margaret was "covered with confusion" (page 193). What does this mean?
3. Outline Mother Margaret Mary's points on obtaining holiness. Choose four key points that you can begin to implement in your own spiritual life.

✝ **Growing in Holiness**

Sister Magdalen des Escures erected a shrine to the Sacred Heart of Jesus, enthroning His Heart in the community. Enthrone a picture of the Sacred Heart of Jesus within your home by making a small shrine with flowers and candles. Frame and hang a list of the Promises of the Sacred Heart near the shrine. (Note that there are twelve promises.) Write a short Act of Consecration as the novices did (page 182), and read it aloud before your shrine. You may also wish to consecrate your entire family to the Sacred Heart of Jesus. Renew these consecrations on the First Friday of each month. (See page 24 of this study guide.)

Begin too to practice the devotion of The Thirty-three Adorations of Jesus Crucified (or of the Cross) in which we are called to adore Him thirty-three times upon the Cross, His throne of mercy—each Friday. These acts of adoration for the conversion of hearts toward Jesus can be made anywhere on Fridays, even while attending to our daily duty. No special formula or vocal prayer is required. A simple look of love or contrition is sufficent.

 Timeline Work

Add the events from 1681 through 1856 to complete your timeline.

Chapters 38 through 41—In Which Jesus Gives the Twelfth Promise, Mother Margaret Mary Helps Others with Her Prayers and Goes to Her Reward

⭐REVIEW⭐ Vocabulary
merely out of *deference*
reigning *sovereign* would be among them
theologian
Seraphim

Comprehension Questions/Narration Prompts
1. What was the twelfth promise to those devoted to the Sacred Heart? What were the problems associated with this promise?
2. After her vision of July 2, 1688, what message about the Sacred Heart of Jesus did Mother Margaret Mary relay?
3. What did Mother Margaret Mary do on her forty-third birthday?
4. What does Mother Margaret Mary suggest to increase the love of God and neighbor?
5. What did Sister Marie Nicole believe to be "the only birthday that matters"?

Forming Opinions/Drawing Conclusions
1. "Any person who has made the nine First Fridays in good faith will never be lost." (page 209) What does this mean?
2. Explain in your own words the situation in England in the late 1680's.

For Further Study
"The writing of letters to so many co-workers took up a great deal of time these days." (page 206) *The Letters of Saint Margaret Mary Alacoque, Apostle of the Sacred Heart* has been republished by Tan Books and Publishers. For greater insight into the soul of St. Margaret Mary, read some of the 142 letters (written between 1678 and 1690) that have been translated into English and compiled in this book.

Conclude your research on seventeenth-century England by studying the Test Acts of 1673 and 1678, the Declaration of Indulgence of King James II (1687), the Glorious Revolution of 1688, the English Bill of Rights of 1689, and Queen Mary II and King William III.

Growing in Holiness
Before the ceremony of the dedication of the Sacred Heart chapel, people walked in procession, singing hymns and chanting litanies (pages 211-12). Pray the Litany of the Sacred Heart of Jesus each First Friday as part of your First Friday devotions. (See page 24 of this study guide.)

Checking the Catechism
Older students may read text paragraphs 790, 1000, 1275, 1391-97, 1419, 1436, and 2837 in the *CCC* (287-292) while younger students review the effects of Holy Communion.

Book Summary Test for *Saint Margaret Mary*

Directions: Answer in complete sentences. If necessary, use the back of the page for additional writing space. (100 possible points, 20 points for each answer)

1. What delayed St. Margaret Mary from fulfilling her call to the religious life? How long was she delayed? What religious order did she choose to join and why?

   _____

   _____

   _____

2. What did Jesus ask St. Margaret Mary to do in order to make reparation for sins committed against the Sacred Heart of Jesus?

   _____

   _____

3. Describe the relationship that St. Margaret Mary had with her superiors as well as the other sisters in her convent? Why did they feel the way they did about her?

   _____

   _____

4. Name at least four of the twelve promises attached to the devotion of the Sacred Heart of Jesus. What must we do in order to obtain these promises?

   _____

   _____

   _____

5. Re-read Chapter 37, "Secrets of Holiness." Consider the acts of reparation that Jesus requested of St. Margaret Mary. What holy habits can you develop to imitate St. Margaret Mary's spirituality and devotion to the Sacred Heart of Jesus?

   _____

   _____

Saint Margaret Mary and the Promises of the Sacred Heart of Jesus
Answer Key to Comprehension Questions

Chapters 1 through 4—In Which Margaret and Her Mother Suffer Illness and Misfortune
1. Margaret's aunts and uncle came to live on the farm with Margaret and her mother after the death of Margaret's father. These relatives, although hard working, were often sharp-tongued and ill tempered toward Margaret and her mother.
2. In Chapter 2, Margaret promises the Blessed Virgin that she will become one of her daughters in a convent if the Blessed Mary would help cure her of the rheumatic fever that she had endured for the past four years. Within several weeks of this promise, Margaret began to recover.
3. The "New Troubles" of Chapter 3 include the difficult work that Margaret was asked to do around the farm, her lack of proper nourishment, and the poor health of her mother.
4. The bothersome problem that worried Margaret was her uncertainty about which convent she should enter when her brother, Philibert, returned to manage the farm.

Chapters 5 through 8—In Which Margaret's Vocation and Mission Begin to Be Understood
1. Margaret's mother had endured many sorrows in the past several years including the poor health of Margaret, her own poor health, and the death of her husband and two of her sons. (She had previously lost two small daughters to death also.) The additional stress leading to her "nervous breakdown" was her son Chrysostom's announcement that he was to be married. Margaret's mother was worried about sharing the household with yet another woman.
2. Margaret wanted to enter a convent in part because she had promised the Blessed Virgin that she would do so in exchange for her cure of rheumatic fever. She also felt that she would "never be happy living in the world" (page 26). At Confirmation she asked the Holy Spirit to grant her the gift of fortitude which she felt she needed to continue to live at home and to set aside her urge to give herself to God in the religious life.
3. The Franciscan friar who conducted a mission in Margaret's parish helped her by convincing her mother and brother that they were offending God by denying Margaret's religious vocation.
4. Margaret did not want to go to the Ursuline convent in Macon as she would be known there. She wanted to go where she would not be known. Margaret felt called to enter the Order of the Visitation of Mary at Paray-le-Monial by the "heavenly voices she so often heard in the depths of her soul" (page 36) and by the fatherly affection of the order's co-founder, St. Francis de Sales.

Chapters 9 through 12—In Which Sister Margaret Mary Encounters Difficulties in the Convent
1. Mother Thouvant explained meditation as "simply turning the mind to one or more spiritual ideas, then asking God for help to think about them profitably" (page 40). The purpose of the reading prior to meditation is to give ideas, or points, for meditation.
2. Mother Hersant summarizes the real vocation of a Visitation nun: "To be extraordinary only by being ordinary" (page 47).
3. Sister Margaret Mary encountered several difficulties in the convent including difficulties in keeping the Rule of the community, problems meditating at the appointed time, and difficulties in completing assigned tasks with timely obedience.
4. Mother de Saumaise was persuaded that Sister Margaret Mary should be allowed to make her Profession as Sister Margaret Mary passed the test of humility that Mother gave her with no signs of defiance. Margaret Mary was professed into the Visitation Order on November 6, 1672.

5. In order to resolve the matter of the visions that Sister Margaret Mary reported, the Visitation superior requested that Margaret Mary write the story of her life, including the presumed visions and a description of the graces she had received since entering the Visitation convent.

Chapters 13 through 16—In Which Sister Margaret Mary Continues to Be Misunderstood

1. On December 27, 1673, our Lord allowed Sister Margaret Mary to feel His yearning for souls when He placed her heart within His own Body. He spoke to her saying, "I have chosen you to make Me known to men" (page 59), thereby making her the Apostle of the Sacred Heart.
2. Both Father Peter and Father Francis expressed to Mother de Saumaise their opinion that Sister Margaret Mary was suffering from mental illness, fatigue, and malnutrition. Their remedy was to fatten up Sister Margaret Mary with vegetable soup. Our Lord consoled Sister Margaret Mary by promising her that He would send her a faithful servant and perfect friend in whom she could confide. He advised her not to be afraid.
3. At His appearance to her during the octave of Corpus Christi in 1674, Christ asked Sister Margaret Mary to receive Him in Holy Communion as often as possible and to make a Holy Hour of Reparation each Thursday night between eleven and twelve o'clock, remaining prostrate throughout this hour.
4. The other sisters reacted negatively to Sister Margaret Mary and her visions. They accused her of being too familiar with our Lord, being prideful in desiring to receive Holy Communion so frequently, and generally disbelieving everything about Sister Margaret Mary's visions.

Chapters 17 through 19—In Which Sister Margaret Mary Continues to Upset the Community, and a New Confessor Arrives

1. Mother de Saumaise gave permission for Sister Margaret Mary to make her Holy Hour and receive Holy Communion on the First Fridays on the condition that she be completely cured of her health problems. This complete restoration of her health would prove that our Lord was appearing to her.
2. The miracle that Mother de Saumaise felt happened at the Visitation convent was the complete cure of Sister Margaret Mary by our Lady who said, "I will restore to you your health according to the Will of my Divine Son" (page 83).
3. Three practices of Sister Margaret Mary that upset the other sisters were her ideas for weekly Holy Hours and reception of Holy Communion on the First Fridays of each month as well as Sister Margaret Mary's "setting herself up above" (page 85) the co-founders of the Visitation Order by suggesting changes within the convent.
4. Father de la Colombière's first impression of Sister Margaret Mary, before he even met her, was that she was a chosen soul.

Chapters 20 through 22—In Which Sister Margaret Mary Finds and Loses a Faithful Friend

1. Sister Margaret Mary was at first unable to confide in Father de la Colombière as she was overwhelmed with fear and self-distrust. She did not feel that Father de la Colombière would be interested and perhaps would not understand her.
2. As explained in the text, "reparation" means "to make up for" (page 97). Our Lord seeks reparation for the people who never consider how much He loves them, and for the general coldness and neglect of all mankind.
3. On June 16, 1675, Father de la Colombière and Sister Margaret Mary consecrated themselves to the service of the Sacred Heart of Jesus. This was in response to our Lord's request to do so on the feast day of the Sacred Heart (the Friday after the octave of Corpus Christi or the Friday after the second Sunday after Pentecost).
4. The two ideas related to the Sacred Heart devotion that were foreign to seventeenth-century Catholics were the ideas of loving God rather than fearing Him, and of receiving Holy Communion frequently.

5. In the fall of 1676, Father de la Colombière was sent to England in order to convert the English monarch, King Charles the Second, and to return the whole country to the Catholic Faith.

Chapters 23 through 25—In Which Our Lord Makes Promises, Letters Arrive from Father de la Colombière, and Sister Margaret Mary Becomes a Victim Soul

1. Mother de Saumaise states that the "all-powerful key that opens Heaven" is patient suffering.
2. Sister Margaret Mary looked upon those who misunderstood and persecuted her without bitterness. She viewed these souls as instruments of God who provided her with many opportunities to suffer.
3. Some of the trials of Mary Beatrice d'Este, the Duchess of York, included her marriage to the much older James, Duke of York, (when she felt called to the Carmelite convent); her residence in the damp climate of England (Her family and friends all lived in Italy.); her maternal care for the Duke's two children; her practice of the Catholic Faith in Protestant England; and the death of her two girls at a young age.
4. The "extremely difficult command" of Chapter 25 is our Lord's request that Sister Margaret Mary offer herself as a victim for the sins of her religious community.

Chapters 26 through 28—In Which Sister Margaret Mary Receives a New Superior, and in England Father De La Colombière Gets Arrested

1. The new superior of the convent, Mother Péronne Rosalie Greyfié, ordered Sister Margaret Mary to discontinue her Holy Hours of Reparation on Thursdays. The prior superior, Mother de Saumaise, had given Sister Margaret Mary permission to make these Holy Hours.
2. Father de la Colombière faced many adversities in England including the marriage of Princess Mary to Prince William of Orange, the death of the Duke and Duchess' baby boy in 1677, his own suffering from tuberculosis, his failure to convert King Charles II, and the danger to his life due to his position as a Catholic clergyman and a Frenchman. He suffered because of the English food and climate, and the tensions between the Protestants and the Catholics in seventeenth-century England. He was arrested on charges of treason and suffered imprisonment.
3. Father de la Colombière believed that true strength for everyone is in the Sacred Heart of Jesus, a treasure house that can never be emptied.
4. Father de la Colombière was arrested on November 24, 1678, on the charges of treason. At this time in England many Catholics were arrested for the so-called Popish Plot to murder the king. The regular actions of Father de la Colombière—making converts to the Faith, offering Mass and administering the sacraments, arranging for young men to study for the priesthood and young girls to be received as religious—were considered actions against the Crown and worthy of death.
5. Instead of wholesome food, warm clothing, or medicine, Father de la Colombière requested that pen, ink, and paper be smuggled into prison for him.

Chapters 29 through 31—In Which Father de la Colombière Returns to France and Comes to the Aid of Sister Margaret Mary

1. The charges made against Father de la Colombière during his court proceeding were that he had plotted to kill King Charles II of England and that he had made Catholic converts in England while furthering the cause of the Pope. The judge held Father de la Colombière over to trial for his life only on the charge that he had made converts to the Catholic Church in England.
2. Father de la Colombière was released from prison on December 21, 1678, as the Duke and Duchess of York had arranged for his release by encouraging the King of France, Louis XIV, to protest. Father de la Colombière was expelled from England and sent back to France.
3. During his two-year stay in England, Father de la Colombière had spread devotion to the Sacred Heart of Jesus and converted many English people to the Catholic faith. He did not,

however, accomplish the original task put to him: the conversion of the English monarch, King Charles II.

Chapters 32 through 34—In Which Father de la Colombière Dies, and More Promises Are Made

1. Father de la Colombière died on February 15, 1682, in Paray-le-Monial, France. He interceded to perform a miracle: King Charles II of England converted to Catholicism before his death in 1685.
2. Mother Melin requested our Lord to immediately grant Sister Margaret Mary perfect health and to let it continue for the next five months so that she might be convinced of Sister Margaret Mary's apparitions. Next, she requested that God would allow Sister Margaret Mary to continue her good health until the end of the year (1683).
3. Several sisters at the Visitation community in Paray-le-Monial expressed concern when Sister Margaret Mary was appointed Novice Mistress. They were fearful that she would concentrate on the devotion to the Sacred Heart at the expense of teaching the novices about the Holy Rule and the writings of the founders of the Visitation Order. They were concerned that the spirit of the order would be lost, and the entire community within the monastery would suffer.
4. The three additional promises of the Sacred Heart that are revealed in Chapter 33 include the following: "I will bless the houses in which the image of My Sacred Heart shall be exposed and honored. I will give to priests the power of moving the most hardened hearts. Persons who propagate this devotion shall have their names inscribed in My Heart, and they shall never be effaced from It" (pages 178-79).
5. For Mother Margaret Mary's feast day, the novices surprised her by preparing a beautiful shrine in honor of the Sacred Heart of Jesus. They each wrote and read a short Act of Consecration to the Sacred Heart and went to the cemetery to pray for the dead.

Chapters 35 through 37—In Which the Other Sisters Begin to Understand Mother Margaret Mary, and She Begins to Teach the Children

1. Mother Melin planned to get the community to accept our Lord's apparitions regarding the devotion to the Sacred Heart by reading Father de la Colombière's book of sermons to them during their meals—their normal time for group spiritual reading. This plan worked so well that after the first reading many of the sisters begged Mother Margaret Mary's forgiveness for their past treatment of her. The Sacred Heart of Jesus was enthroned in the community, and plans were undertaken to build a chapel to the Sacred Heart of Jesus on the convent's grounds.
2. The Feast of the Sacred Heart was celebrated in the Visitation convent at Paray-le-Monial on the first Friday after the feast of Corpus Christi, the day chosen by our Lord Himself in 1673. This feast continues to be celebrated today by the entire Catholic Church.
3. The sisters changed their hearts toward Mother Margaret Mary after hearing of Father de la Colombière's support of the devotion to the Sacred Heart in his book of sermons that was read to the entire community. Within this book, Father de la Colombière referred to a certain person (Mother Margaret Mary) who had enlightened him on what he should say and write.
4. Early in 1687, Mother Margaret Mary was appointed as Mistress of Pupils and received charge of the instruction of the girls within the school attached to the monastery.
5. Mother Margaret Mary's definition of a saint is simply a person who always says "Yes" to God's Will. (See page 201 for more specifics.) According to Mother Margaret Mary, the "key to holiness" is to love God, as well as our neighbor, very much.

Chapters 38 through 41—In Which Jesus Gives the Twelfth Promise, Mother Margaret Mary Helps Others with Her Prayers, and Goes to Her Reward

1. The twelfth and last promise our Lord made to those devoted to the Sacred Heart was the greatest promise: "I promise you, in the excessive mercy of My Heart, that Its all-powerful love will grant to all those who communicate on the First Friday of every month for nine consecutive months the grace of final repentance. They shall not die in Its disfavor, nor without receiving their sacraments, and My Divine Heart will be their assured refuge at the

last moment" (page 207). The problems that this promise presented were in the meaning of the phrase "their sacraments," and the possibilities that a person—after receiving Holy Communion for nine consecutive months—may become lax about his spiritual life or completely drift into a life of mortal sin, dying in that state.
2. After her vision of July 2, 1688, Mother Margaret Mary relayed the Lord's message: "Henceforth the Visitation Order would have the task of making devotion to the Sacred Heart known and loved throughout the world, assisted by the Fathers and Brothers of the Society of Jesus" (page 211).
3. On her forty-third birthday, Mother Margaret Mary began "a forty-day retreat in preparation for her death" (page 217).
4. To increase the love of God and neighbor (and make the world less of a cold and lonely place), Mother Margaret Mary suggested to Sister Marie Nicole that people receive Holy Communion more often, especially on the First Fridays.
5. Sister Marie Nicole stated that "the only birthday that matters" is our death, our entrance into eternal joy.

Answer Key to Book Summary Test

1. St. Margaret Mary's call to the religious life was delayed for more than ten years, first of all by her brothers' educations and secondly by her family's reluctance to grant permission for her to enter the convent. When she was finally given permission, she chose the Order of the Visitation convent in Paray-le-Monial. She felt called by our Lord, the Blessed Virgin, and the order's founder St. Francis de Sales to join this order—an order founded for prayer and reparation.
2. Jesus asked St. Margaret Mary to make a Holy Hour of Reparation every Thursday night between eleven and twelve o'clock, remaining prostrate throughout this hour. In addition, He requested that she receive Holy Communion as often as possible, especially on the First Friday of every month in order to make reparation for the many sins committed against the Sacred Heart of Jesus.
3. St. Margaret Mary had a difficult relationship with many of her peers in the convent as well as her superiors. For many years, St. Margaret Mary was believed to be mentally ill. She was persecuted and ridiculed as it is difficult for people to believe that someone they know well—someone they believe to be an ordinary person—would be the recipient of visions from our Lord. Many of St. Margaret Mary's superiors and peers were unable to accept this different sister. They expected and pressured her to act and believe like all the other sisters did without promoting new ideas and devotions that were not already written into the rule of their order.
4. Jesus made the Twelve Promises of the Sacred Heart to St. Margaret Mary for all those who would honor His Sacred Heart. The last promise applies to those who receive Holy Communion on the First Friday of the month for nine consecutive months: 1. I will give them all the graces necessary for their state of life. 2. I will establish peace in their families. 3. I will console them in all their difficulties. 4. I will be their assured refuge in life, and more especially at death. 5. I will pour out abundant benedictions on all their undertakings. 6. Sinners will find in My Heart a source and infinite ocean of mercy. 7. Tepid souls shall become more fervent. 8. Fervent souls shall advance rapidly to great perfection. 9. I will bless the houses in which the image of My Sacred Heart shall be exposed and honored. 10. I will give to priests the power of moving the most hardened hearts. 11. Persons who propagate this devotion shall have their names inscribed in My Heart, and they shall never be effaced from It. 12. I promise you, in the excessive mercy of My Heart, that Its all-powerful love will grant to all those who communicate on the First Friday of every month for nine consecutive months the grace of final repentance. They shall not die in Its disfavor, nor without receiving their sacraments, and My Divine Heart will be their assured refuge at the last moment.
5. Answers will vary.

Prayers to the Sacred Heart of Jesus

Litany: "Lord, have mercy on us. *Christ, have mercy on us.* Lord, have mercy on us. Christ, hear us. *Christ, graciously hear us.* (Each of the following invocations lead by the leader is followed by all saying "*have mercy on us.*"*) God the Father of Heaven, *. God the Son, Redeemer of the world, *. God the Holy Spirit, *. Holy Trinity one God, *. Heart of Jesus, Son of the Eternal Father, *. Heart of Jesus, formed by the Holy Spirit in the Virgin Mother's womb, *. Heart of Jesus, substantially united to the Word of God, *. Heart of Jesus, of infinite majesty, *. Heart of Jesus, holy temple of God, *. Heart of Jesus, rich unto all who call upon You, *. Heart of Jesus, fount of life and holiness, *. Heart of Jesus, propitiation for our offenses, *. Heart of Jesus, overwhelmed with reproaches, *. Heart of Jesus, bruised for our iniquities, *. Heart of Jesus, obedient even unto death, *. Heart of Jesus, pierced with a lance, *. Heart of Jesus, source of all consolation, *. Heart of Jesus, our life and resurrection, *. Heart of Jesus, our peace and reconciliation, *. Heart of Jesus, victim for sins, *. Heart of Jesus, salvation of those who hope in You, *. Heart of Jesus, hope of those who die in You, *. Heart of Jesus, Delight of all saints, *. Lamb of God, Who takes away the sins of the world, *Spare us, O Lord*. Lamb of God, Who takes away the sins of the world, *Graciously hear us, O Lord*. Lamb of God, Who takes away the sins of the world, *Have mercy on us*. Jesus, meek and humble of Heart, *Please make our hearts like unto Your own*. Let us pray: Almighty and everlasting God, look upon the Heart of Your well-beloved Son and upon the praise and satisfaction which He offers You in the name of sinners; and in Your goodness, grant them pardon when they seek Your mercy, in the Name of Your Son, Jesus Christ, Who lives and reigns with You forever and ever. Amen."

Offering/Consecration: "Sacred Heart of Jesus, I give myself to You. I give You my body, my soul, and all that I do or think or say. I want my whole life to be an offering to You to make You known and loved. I also offer to You our family. Help us to obey and love you always. Keep us from all danger of soul and body. Bless our life together with Your peace and love. We hope for the forgiveness of our sins through Your mercy, and for the graces we need to save our souls. Through Holy Communion and prayer, keep us close to Your Sacred Heart. Sacred Heart of Jesus, we believe in Your Love for us. Help us to love You more. Amen."

Novena Prayer of St. Pio of Pietrelcina: "O My Jesus, You have said, 'Truly I say to you, ask and it will be given you, seek and you will find, knock and it will be opened to you.' Behold, I knock, I seek, and I ask for the grace of . . ." (*Our Father . . . Hail Mary . . . Glory Be . . .* Sacred Heart of Jesus, I place all my trust in You.) "O my Jesus, You have said: 'Truly I say to you, if you ask anything of the Father in My Name, He will give it to you.' Behold, in Your name, I ask the Father for the grace of . . ." (*Our Father . . . etc.*) "O my Jesus, You have said: 'Truly I say to you, heaven and earth will pass away, but My words will not pass away.' Encouraged by Your infallible words, I now ask for the grace of . . ." (*Our Father . . . etc.*) O Sacred Heart of Jesus, for whom it is impossible not to have compassion on the afflicted, have mercy on us sinners, and grant us the grace which we ask of You, through the Sorrowful and Immaculate Heart of Mary, Your tender mother and ours. *Hail Holy Queen . . .*" St. Joseph, foster father of Jesus, pray for us." Amen.

Invocations: "Most Sacred Heart of Jesus, have mercy on us. Sweet Heart of Jesus, I put my trust in You." "Heart of Jesus, burning with love for us, set our hearts on fire with love of You." "Jesus, meek and humble of heart, make our hearts like unto Thine" "All for You, Most Sacred Heart of Jesus!" "Sacred Heart of Jesus, may You be known, loved, and imitated." "Sweet Heart of Jesus, be my love." "Sacred Heart of Jesus, make me love You and make you loved!"

Study Guide for

Saint Francis Solano, Wonder-Worker of the New World and Apostle of Argentina and Peru

St. Francis Solano

St. Francis Solano was born upper class.
With music and singing, much time would he pass.
Kind, generous was he.
A priest he would be.
Not riches but graces he wished to amass.

Delays did not upset him, in tune with God's will.
A teacher of others, God's love did instill.
Good works and prayer,
Cures were his flair.
Esteem he sought not, but it came to him still.

Franciscan he was, to Africa he willed—
To convert many souls, God's kingdom to build.
His superiors declined,
Other jobs assigned.
Music, preaching, and curing, in these he was skilled.

And then to Peru he traveled on ships.
Storm, shipwreck, conversions, maroonment, hardships.
Peacefully he bore
What God had in store.
"God be praised" were the words ever on his lips.

He converted the natives, walked many miles.
Spoke all the languages, regardless of styles.
With cross, violin,
Many battles did win.
His love of suffering overcame many trials.

Great sermons he preached, made miracles occur.
Wherever he traveled, he caused quite a stir.
He disliked his fame,
Did all in God's name.
"Wonder-worker of Peru," this title we confer.

Think what you can learn from this saint and his tale.
How you can apply it to help you prevail.
Then mold what you do
And boldly pursue
His pattern of holiness. Follow his trail.

Timeline of Events

Year	Event
1533	Francisco Pizarro captures the Inca capital, Cuzco, and conquers Peru
1535	Silver mines discovered in Peru; city of Trujillo founded; St. Thomas More beheaded
1549	Birth of Francis Solano (Solanus) March 10, 1549, at Montilla, Spain, to Matthew Sanchez Solanus and Anna Ximenes, Andalusian nobles
1551	Founding of the first university in the New World at Lima, Peru
1552	St. Francis Xavier dies; war breaks out between Spain and France (to 1556)
1564	Wm. Shakespeare born; death of Michelangelo; Christopher Marlowe born
1566	Francis Solanus decides to pursue his priestly vocation; Nostradamus dies
1569	Francis Solano joins the Alcantrine Franciscans
1570	April 25th—Francis Solano's Profession Day, formally joins order
1576	Francis Solano ordained a priest; introduction of decimal fractions
1579	Martin de Porres born; St. John of the Cross writes "Dark Night of the Soul"
1580	Francis Solano appointed Novice Master for the convent in Montoro, Spain
1582	Francis Solano appointed Father Guardian; Gregorian Calendar, named for Pope Gregory XIII, adopted by Papal States; death of Teresa of Avila
1583	Francis heroically ministers during the plague at Montoro; contracts the disease himself but recovers; death of Francis' friend Father Bonaventure
1584	Francis transferred to the Friary of St. Louis in Granada, Spain; death of St. Charles Borromeo; Sir Walter Raleigh discovers Virginia
1585	Birth of St. John Masias; "War of Three Henries" starts in France
1586	Birth of St. Rose in Lima, Peru; the Jesuits found missions in Paraguay
1589	Francis arrives in South America with Father Balthazar Navarro to serve as a missionary; forks used for first time at French court
1590	Francis arrives in Peru and begins missionary work in Talavera; first microscope made by Hans and Zacharias Janssen; Shakespeare writes "Henry VI"
1595	Death of St. Philip Neri; first appearance of heels on shoes
1599	Birth of Blessed Marie Guyard of New France; Oliver Cromwell born
1602	Francis arrives in Lima, Peru, in June as Vicar of the Friary of St. Mary of the Angels; he is appointed Father Guardian and several months later, is transferred to Trujillo; Galileo investigates law of gravitation
1604	Francis reappointed as Father Guardian at the Friary of St. Mary of the Angels; delivers his "great sermon" in December; Russians settle in Siberia
1606	Death of Turibius Alphonsus de Mogrovejo on March 23rd; Francis transferred to the less strict friary of San Francisco as a simple friar where he continues his street preaching until May 1610; discovery of Australia
1610	Death of Francis Solano on July 14 in Lima, Peru; first telescope observations made by Galileo; death of King Henry IV of Navarre, France
1617	St. Rose of Lima dies; Pocahontas dies; St. Alphonsus Rodriguez dies
1626	Rebuilding of St. Peter's Basilica in Rome completed; Francis Bacon dies
1639	Death of St. Martin de Porres; Rembrandt paints portrait of his mother
1645	Death of St. John Masias; Battle of Naseby on June 14th (English Civil War)
1675	Francis Solano was beatified by Pope Clement X on June 20, 1675, and canonized by Pope Benedict XIII on December 27, 1726

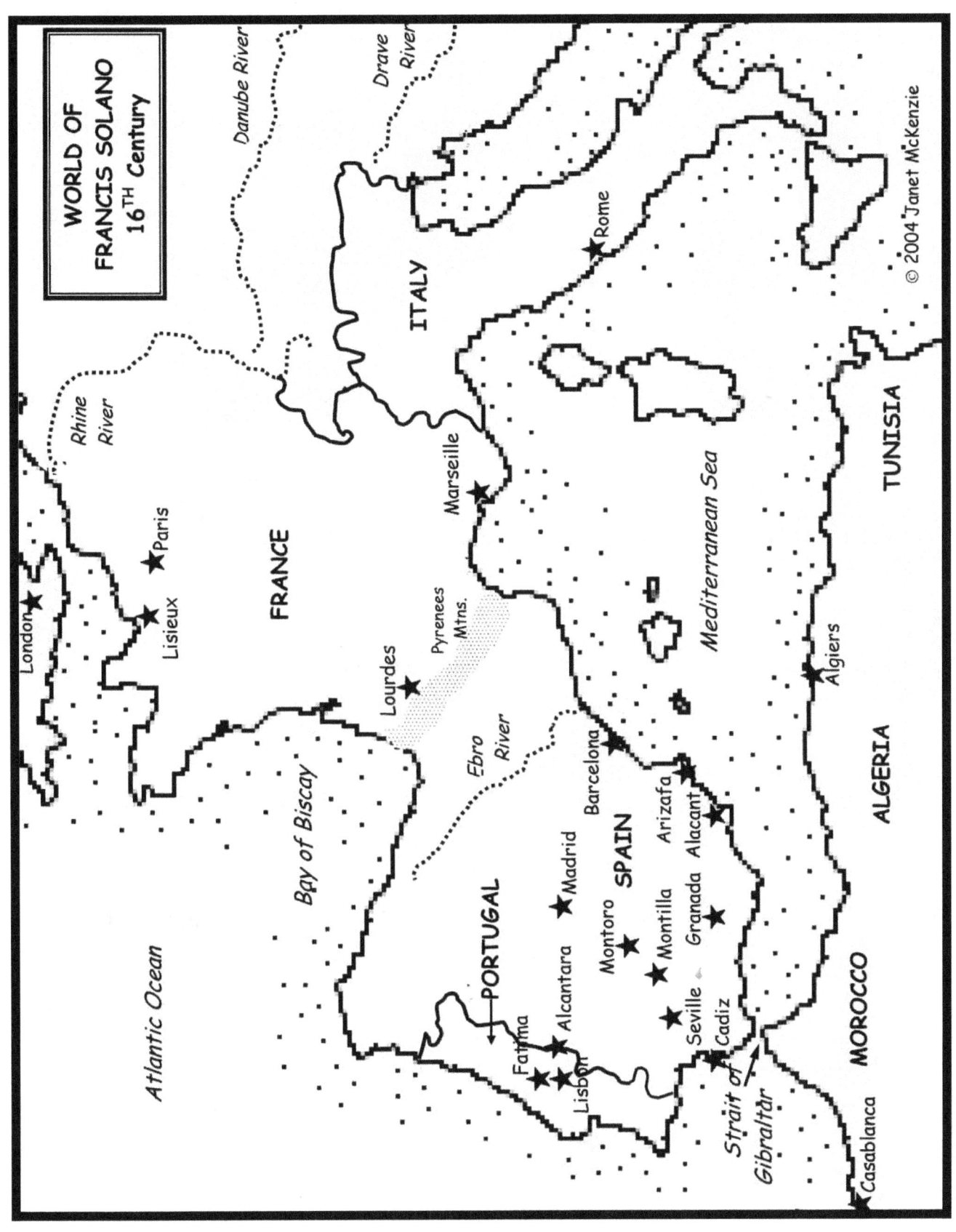

Chapter 1–In Which We Meet Francis Solano, the Mayor's Son

 Vocabulary

if this *blackguard* hadn't insulted [me] *friary*
an elderly *vagabond* came into view God's Providence (Providence of God)

 Comprehension Questions/Narration Prompts
5. What two reasons does Francis give for wanting to become a Franciscan?
6. Francis refused to play ball with the other students as he had "important business" that day. What was this business?
7. What does Francis believe is the best way to fulfill God's Will?

 Forming Opinions/Drawing Conclusions
1. What prompted Francis to intervene in the duel between the two strangers? What virtues does this demonstrate? Is this something you might have done? Explain.
2. What does the following phrase mean: "Friendship is a foretaste of Heaven" (page 8)?

 Growing in Holiness
In His sermon on the mount in Matthew 5, Jesus talked about the reward peacemakers would receive. Look for opportunities to live out this beatitude, especially within your own family. Become a peacemaker in imitation of St. Francis Solano.

 Geography
Trace the map of Europe found on page 27 of this study guide. Label and color the four bodies of water blue as well as the four rivers. Label the Pyrenees Mountains and color them brown. (This map will be completed in Chapter 6.)

✓ **Checking the Catechism**
Older students may review the teachings of the *Catechism of the Catholic Church* (*CCC*) regarding the beatitudes and our desire for happiness in text paragraphs 1716-1728 (359-362). What beatitudes does Francis demonstrate in this chapter? Younger students may study references to the beatitudes in their own catechisms. Study also why God made us.

 Searching Scripture
1. Read Jesus' Sermon on the Mount (or Plain) as recorded in Matthew (5:1-12) and Luke (6:20-26). Note that Matthew's passage contains nine blessings, and Luke's contains four blessings and four curses.
2. Francis sings a hymn to the Queen of Peace. Research in Holy Scripture the references to peace such as Isaiah 9:6 (Isaias 9:5), Prince of Peace; Luke 24:36, peace Jesus gives; and Philippians 4:4-7, peace of God.

Chapter 2–In Which Francis Receives the Habit and Counsels His Friend

 Vocabulary

speak these words so *glibly*
Francis would be *scandalized*
Father Guardian
Novice Master

 Comprehension Questions/Narration Prompts
1. Why was Francis required to delay his entrance into the religious life?
2. To whom is the grace of emptying our hearts in order to hold Christ given?
3. When did the Franciscan friars accept Francis Solano as a novice?

 Forming Opinions/Drawing Conclusions
1. Explain Francis' talk of "tools, and chalices and emptied hearts" (page 14).
2. What are some things you can do—or abstain from doing—to help open your heart to Christ, enabling you to become a chalice for Christ?
3. Why did Father Peter send Friar John to speak to Francis?
4. Do you believe that some people can perceive the presence of evil? How can you sharpen your sense of evil in order to avoid its influence?

 For Further Study
1. Research the Alcantrine Franciscans and their founder, St. Peter of Alcantara (1499-1562). What saints did St. Peter of Alcantara counsel? Research the life of another great Alcantrine Franciscan, St. Paschal Baylon.
2. John refers to the "New World" (page 20). Research sixteenth-century New World explorers: Sebastian Cabot, Jacques Cartier, Sir Francis Drake, and Ferdinand Magellan.

 Growing in Holiness
Implement those ideas you had that would allow yourself to become a chalice for Christ. Try extra prayers, fasting, and any other action that will strengthen your Will in order to become more open to the Will of God.

 **Timeline Work**
Taping sheets of plain paper end-to-end, make a timeline representing the years from 1533 through 1675. Let three inches equal 25 years. Mark on your timeline the dates and events from 1533 through 1569, using information from page 26 of this study guide.

✓ **Checking the Catechism**
Older students may read the Church's teaching on avoiding evil in text paragraphs 1806, 1889, 1950, 1962, and 2527 (57-58, 363, 372, 375-376, and 597) of the *Catechism of the Catholic Church* (*CCC*).

Chapter 3—In Which Francis Tells Us His Secret to Holiness

 Vocabulary

glowing now with a *myriad* of stars
Francis turned *impulsively*

Profession Day
redemption

 Comprehension Questions/Narration Prompts
1. For what grace did Francis pray on behalf of his friend John?
2. What does the Father Guardian state is the "best coin with which to ransom sinners"? (page 23)
3. Where was Francis' new cell located in the friary of Seville?
4. What does Francis believe is the "best prayer a human being can offer"? (page 26)

 Forming Opinions/Drawing Conclusions
1. Do you believe that if Francis had prayed harder or better that John would have stayed with the Franciscans? Does God always answer our prayers as we want them answered?
2. What does Francis mean when he says, "Our *wills* must be crucified" (page 30)?
3. Summarize Francis' secret regarding the Holy Sacrifice of the Mass. How can you use this secret to increase your own holiness?

 Growing in Holiness
1. ". . . this meant accepting pain and disappointment in a cheerful spirit . . ." (page 29). In imitation of St. Francis Solano, ask your guardian angel to help you become more cheerful in sacrifice, in disappointment, and in the exercise of your daily duty.
2. In honor of Jesus in the tabernacle, begin the practice of reciting the Prayer of St. Francis (top of page 26) whenever passing a Catholic Church.

✓ **Checking the Catechism**

Younger students may study the Holy Sacrifice of the Mass in their catechisms. Older students may read text paragraphs 616-623 and 1402-1405 (271, 275, and 280-281) in the *CCC* on the Mass. If desired, complete Activities #49-51 in *100 Activities Based on the Catechism of the Catholic Church* (*100 Activities*).

 Searching Scripture
1. ". . . the smallest hints of the good things which God has in store for those who serve Him faithfully" (page 24). Read 1 Corinthians 2:9-10.
2. ". . . make our wills like His" (page 30). Read Matthew 5:48.

Chapter 4–In Which Father Francis Continues to Glorify God in His Work

 Vocabulary

as for the empty *larder*
covered with *hideous* ulcers

Conventual Mass
Gospel

 Comprehension Questions/Narration Prompts
1. What new job did the Father Guardian give to Francis in the year 1576?
2. According to Father Francis, what is "all that matters" (page 35)?
3. Why did Father Francis return to the Montilla friary? What was his assignment there?
4. The younger friars were in awe of one of Francis' gifts, "Surely if he had stayed in the world he would have made a great name for himself" (page 37). What was this gift?

 Forming Opinions/Drawing Conclusions
1. After nine years as a Franciscan, Father Francis still had not been assigned to the job that was in his heart. What was this job? What allowed Francis to continue to be at peace with his vocation despite this disappointment?
2. What do you think will be the effect of Francis' prayerful reading of the passage of John's Gospel?

 For Further Study
Research the situation between the Christians and those who followed the teaching of Mohammed during the sixteenth century.

 Growing in Holiness
Today, and every day for the rest of your life, ask for "the grace of being completely united to God's Will" (page 40). End every prayer of petition with this submission, "if it be Your Holy Will." No task is too small, too boring, or too unfulfilling if done out of obedience or for the greater glory of God.

✓ **Checking the Catechism**
Older students may read text paragraphs 1096, 1174-78, 1437, and 2691 (243 and 567) in the *CCC* on the Liturgy of the Hours (Divine Hours). If desired, complete Activity #85, "The Liturgy of the Hours" (Divine Office), in *100 Activities*.

📖 **Searching Scripture**
Francis speaks of using our gifts for the glory of God (page 35). Read these Scriptural passages: Isaiah (Isaias) 43:7, John 17:4, 1 Corinthians 10:31, 1 Peter 4:10, and Revelation (Apocalypse) 4:11. Also read Luke 7:11-17 regarding Jesus' encounter with a woman's only son.

Chapter 5–In Which Father Francis Teaches His Novices Valuable Lessons

 Vocabulary

have the *inestimable* advantage
those *stalwart* men

Carmelite
litanies (litany)

 Comprehension Questions/Narration Prompts
1. After applying for a transfer, where was Father Francis sent? What was his new assignment there?
2. What analogy or comparison did Father Francis use to teach his novices about growing in the service of God?
3. What additional job did Francis acquire when the novitiate was transferred to San Francisco del Monte? To what new position was he elected two years later?

 Forming Opinions/Drawing Conclusions
1. Summarize the miracles attributed to the intercession of St. Francis Solano in this chapter.
2. Explain this quotation of St. Teresa of Avila: "One perfect soul can do more for God's glory than a thousand ordinary souls" (page 46).

 For Further Study
Research the life of St. Teresa of Jesus (1515-1582) who was responsible for the reform of the Carmelite cloistered nuns.

 Growing in Holiness
1. We too share Friar Philip's source of discouragement: pride (page 47). It takes time, patience, and much work to become a saint. Do not get discouraged as you travel your spiritual journey. Continue to take small steps of progress. Often our progress is greater than we may think.
2. Trials "become less painful if one meets them with a smile" (page 49). Begin to practice smile mortification every day. When something unpleasant happens, "Smile not for yourself, but for Him" (page 50). Ask your guardian angel to help you to be cheerful on the outside even when you do not feel cheerful inside.

Searching Scripture
1. Read more parables that relate to plants and gardening, as well as the purpose of parables in Matthew Chapters 12 and 13.
2. "I would rather have had the least place in the house . . ." (page 52). Read Proverbs 25:6-7 and Luke 14:7-11.

Chapter 6–In Which Father Francis Endangers His Life to Fight the Plague

 Vocabulary

seized with a strange *palsy*
the parish priest had *succumbed*
vestry
Tabernacle

 Comprehension Questions/Narration Prompts
1. What did the citizens of Montoro do in an effort to stem the progress of the plague?
2. How did Father Francis organize the townspeople in order to fight the plague more effectively?

 Forming Opinions/Drawing Conclusions
1. Why were the townspeople of Montoro so afraid of the plague?
2. Why did Father Francis try to divert the townspeople's gratitude for him to Father Bonaventure? Read Philippians 2:3-4.

 For Further Study
Although the plague (initially known as the bubonic plague or Black Death and later changed to the pneumonic plague) reached its peak in Europe during the fourteenth century, it was still common during the sixteenth century. Reseach this disease which often killed its victims within hours and was responsible for over 25 million deaths in Europe alone.

 Growing in Holiness
"Oh, Father, increase our faith and courage!" (page 60). Pray each day that God will increase your faith in him, your trust in him, your love of him and your neighbor, and your courage to live out your faith against trial and temptation. Ask God daily to increase your desire to give him glory.

 Geography
Complete the map started in Chapter 1 by labeling all cities red and the countries green. On the map provided, cities are indicated with a star; countries are in bold capitals.

✓ **Checking the Catechism**
"We give ourselves to You as little children. . . . Give Yourself to us as a true Father" (page 60). Older students may read what the *CCC* teaches about the children of God in the following text paragraphs: 1, 52, 270, 422, 654, 1709, and 2009 (1, 147, 258, and 357).

Chapter 7–In Which Francis Becomes a Missionary at Last

 Vocabulary

fallen ill of the dreadful *malady*
Indians . . . had many *dialects*

Father Provincial (or Provincial)
True Faith

 Comprehension Questions/Narration Prompts
1. What had Father Bonaventure proved by his heroic actions throughout the plague?
2. Why did Francis wish to leave his post in Montoro?
3. After five years in Granada, what was Francis' new assignment?
4. What conditions or circumstances made the job of the missionaries in South America difficult?

 Forming Opinions/Drawing Conclusions
1. Why do you suppose that Father Francis believed prayer for Father Bonaventure to be futile?
2. Explain the dying words of Father Bonaventure as found at the top of page 66.

 For Further Study

Research the following people mentioned briefly in this chapter: King Philip II of Spain who reigned from 1556-1598 and the Spanish explorer Don Francisco Pizarro (1474-1541).

 Growing in Holiness

"But what was the use of worrying" (page 77)? The Curé of Ars, St. John Vianney, stated, "God commands you to pray, but He forbids you to worry." Reflect on this wisdom in light of the teachings of these saints as well as the following passages from the Bible: 1 Thessalonians 5:17 and Matthew 6:27.

 Geography

Trace the map of South America from page 28 of this study guide. Label and color the sea, gulfs, and oceans blue. Draw and color the Amazon River blue. Draw and color the Andes Mountains brown. Label the countries (indicated in bold capitals) in green. Copy the dashed black line for the equator.

Timeline Work

Add the dates and events from 1570 through 1589 to your timeline.

Chapter 8–In Which Father Francis Saves Many Souls at Sea

Vocabulary
no waterway through the *Isthmus*
with a *motley* group of soldiers
general absolution
Sanctifying Grace

Comprehension Questions/Narration Prompts
1. Who were the first missionary students of Father Francis?
2. What prompted the baptism of hundreds of souls aboard the ship in which Francis and his companions sailed?
3. What did Francis do in an attempt to add force to his prayers to stop the storm at sea?
4. How did Francis alert the men on shore and let them know that men were still alive on board the half-ship?

Forming Opinions/Drawing Conclusions
1. In your own words, retell the story of Father Francis' trip from Cartagena to the Gulf of Gorgona.
2. Name the three miracles that happened at sea with Father Francis.

For Further Study
In 1589 when St. Francis Solano traveled through the Isthmus of Panama, there was no canal to aid in crossing from the Caribbean Sea to the Pacific Ocean. Research the history of the Panama Canal. When was the canal completed? Who now owns the canal?

Growing in Holiness
As Father Francis watched men drowning in the sea, he offered a classic prayer for the dead (page 87). Memorize this prayer and pray it daily for the Holy Souls in Purgatory.

Geography
Track the trip of Francis and his companions on the map of South America by marking the journey in purple. (Use dashed lines for sea travel.) Begin with the stop in Cartagena, the crossing of the Gulf of Darien to Panama, across to the Pacific Ocean and down the western coast of the continent to the Gulf of Gorgona. Label the cities of Callao, Lima, and Buenaventura in red.

Checking the Catechism
Older students may read text paragraph 1483 (311) in the *CCC* regarding the conditions for the use and reception of general absolution.

Chapter 9–In Which Father Francis and His Companions Are Stranded on the Shore

 Vocabulary

spirits were at a low *ebb*
fish . . . caught in a *lagoon*

Our Father (Pater Noster)
shrine

 Comprehension Questions/Narration Prompts
1. What important item did Father Francis lose as he got on the rescue boat?
2. What action did Father Balthazar take to help the situation of the stranded survivors?
3. How did Father Francis distract the sailors after Father Balthazar left?

 Forming Opinions/Drawing Conclusions
1. Explain the various "troubles" on the shore. In your opinion, which of these troubles will be the biggest one for Father Francis and his companions to overcome?
2. Make a prediction about what will happen next to Father Francis and his companions. If you were one of the stranded survivors, what kind of a plan would you make in case Father Balthazar does not return?

 Growing in Holiness
1. Father Francis and his companions construct an outdoor shrine to house a statue of our Lady. If you do not have such a shrine in your yard now, design and build a protective cover for an outdoor shrine in order that the Blessed Mother may be honored in your yard. You may include decorative flowers and plants just as Francis' men did.
2. The sailors brought all of their food to Father Francis for his blessing before it was eaten. Offer a blessing over all of the food that you eat. It is a holy practice to make the Sign of the Cross over even a glass of water in order to constantly remind ourselves that all of our nourishment is a gift from God. Each day ask God to watch over the millions of people who will not get enough food today to take care of their basic nutritional needs.

✓ **Checking the Catechism**
"Francis began to recite the *Our Father*" (page 91). Younger children may study the Our Father as explained their catechisms. Older students may read the following summary text paragraphs in the *CCC*: 2773-2776, 2797-2802, and 2857-2865 (578-598). If desired, complete Activity #97 in *100 Activities*.

 Searching Scripture
Fathers Didacus Pineda and Francis Torres cooked some fish on the shore. Read a similar story in Holy Scripture in John 21:1-14.

Chapter 10–In Which Francis and His Companions Arrive in Lima

 Vocabulary

after much *arduous* journeying
he muttered *petulantly*

episcopal
alms

 Comprehension Questions/Narration Prompts
1. What happened to the men who disobeyed the order that all food must be blessed by Father Francis before it was eaten?
2. Why did Father Francis and his companions travel along the shoreline as they began their 600-mile walk from Payta to Lima?
3. Who did Father Francis and his companions hope to meet in Lima? Who did Father Francis meet while there?

 Forming Opinions/Drawing Conclusions
1. Retell the story of Chan Chan and the Incans.
2. How does Father Francis define a foolish man? Do you agree? Do you, or anyone you know, fall into that category?

 For Further Study
1. Research the Incan civilization of Peru, which was centered in Cuzco. The Incan empire was founded in 1220 and was well established by the fifteenth century. Study their farming methods as well as their extensive road system. What is the Chimu Empire?
2. Find out more information on Archbishop Turbius (Toribio) Alphonsus de Mogrovejo, St. Rose of Lima, St. Martin de Porres, and St. John Masias. Is the Archbishop also a saint?

 Growing in Holiness
"Let us praise God in song" (page 102). St. Augustine said, "He who sings, prays twice." Praise God in song each day. The Psalms originally were written as songs of praise to be used in the temple. Many of the lyrics of our Catholic hymns are taken from the psalms. Even if you feel your voice does not praise God, you can pray the psalms.

Geography
1. Continue to track the southward journey of Francis and his companions on the map of South America. Your purple line should now extend from Cartagena, Columbia, to Lima, Peru. Label these cities in red: Trujillo, Guayaquil, Nazca, Huancayo, Cuzco, and Payta.
2. Draw in dashed lines on the map the extent of the Incan empire during its height around 1525.

Chapter 11–In Which Father Francis Learns about the Indians of Socotonio

 Vocabulary

llamas and *alpacas*
they *plied* their various skills

superior
Francis of Assisi

 Comprehension Questions/Narration Prompts
1. What reasons did John give to explain why he no longer desired to be a priest?
2. What ability of Father Francis' amazed the governor, Don Andres?
3. According to Father Francis, who is the Franciscan patron saint of students?

 Forming Opinions/Drawing Conclusions
1. Why was John not happy? Explain how pride had contributed to his unhappiness.
2. Why did Father Francis change his mind about the importance of John coming back to the priesthood?
3. Summarize Francis' discussion with Don Andres on prayer. How can the proper attitude about prayer lead to true peace?
4. Predict what Francis will do with the stick he requested from Father John.

 For Further Study
Research the life of St. Bonaventure who lived from 1221 to 1274. He was inscribed as one of the Doctors of the Church. Find out which other saint received his doctoral university degree with St. Bonaventure.

 Growing in Holiness
St. Francis Solano suggests that each petition we make be accompanied with the petition that we may grow in real knowledge and love of the Heavenly Father and His Will. Pray daily to obtain these graces.

 Geography
On the map of South America, draw Father Francis' journey from Lima to Talavera in purple. Label the following cities in red: Potosi, Arica, Tucumán, Talavera, Santiago del Estero, and (New) Córdoba.

✓ **Checking the Catechism**
Francis wants us to beg each day to grow in knowledge and love of God's Will. Older students can read more about the Will of God in the *CCC* by reading the following text paragraphs: 51, 295, 541, 763, and 2822-27 (55, 91, 121, and 591). Younger students should study the requirements of gaining the happiness of heaven.

Chapter 12–In Which Father Francis Makes Friends with the Pagan Tribes

⟨REVIEW⟩ Vocabulary
much *averse* to settling down
what they considered to be *treachery*

Provincial Chapter (chapter)
Custos

??? Comprehension Questions/Narration Prompts
1. What did Father Francis do with the stick he obtained from Father John?
2. By what new method did the inhabitants of Socotonio grind their grain?
3. By what title did Francis become known? Why was this title given to him?
4. What new appointment was given to Father Francis in 1595?
5. What two weapons did Father Francis take with him to meet the pagan tribe whose leader was Peter Cotero?
6. What gift had God in His infinite mercy given Father Francis so that he might be an effecttive missionary?

Forming Opinions/Drawing Conclusions
1. Explain this expression from page 130, "Francis' zeal for souls."
2. How are these two descriptions of Father Francis from page 131 connected, "Inflamed with love of God and souls to an intense degree (and so a man of constant prayer and penance)"?

For Further Study
Father Francis Solano worked hard to spread Christianity to the pagan tribes in South America. Earlier in the sixteenth century, our Blessed Mother appeared in Mexico asking that a church be built to help bring Christianity to the pagan people of central America. Research the appearance of Our Lady of Guadalupe to St. Juan Diego in 1531.

Growing in Holiness
A crucifix and violin were Father Francis' "weapons" when he encountered his enemies. How do you approach people who might react to you defensively? What "weapons" do you use to befriend people? How can you better imitate St. Francis Solano in this regard?

Searching Scripture
The mayor stated, "This good priest is a saint and has the gift of tongues—just like the Apostles" (page 136). Also known as *glossolalia*, this gift allows the speaker to be understood by all, even if the hearers speak a different language. Read about a different gift of tongues—that described by St. Paul in the early Church as unintelligible speech—in 1 Corinthians 14:1-40. This gift of tongues is present in modern times as well.

Chapter 13–In Which Father Francis Converts a Great Many Souls

 Vocabulary

destruction and *plunder* *Commissary General*
reveling in the new opportunity *penance*

 Comprehension Questions/Narration Prompts
1. How many warriors did Father Francis convert on that Holy Thursday?
2. What did Father Francis claim is the secret of the Christian life?
3. List the three appointments Father Francis received in this chapter.

 Forming Opinions/Drawing Conclusions
1. Retell the story of Francis' conversion of the attacking warriors in Rioja.
2. Father Francis found it easier to obey than to give orders. Which is easier for you? List the advantages and disadvantages of each.
3. Explain the following quotation from St. Francis Solano: "Suffering is hard only when we try to escape from it, not when we go out freely to meet it" (page 150).
4. Why was Father Francis given the title of "Wonder-Worker"? Support your answer with specific examples from this chapter.

 Growing in Holiness
Ask God to grant you a love of suffering to help you die to your own will and win many souls for heaven. We must desire to do good works and to suffer. St. Augustine states, "The entire life of a good Christian is an exercise in holy desire." Ask God to grant you the desire to please him in all things.

 Geography
Father Francis traveled the 1,400-mile journey from Tucumán to Lima by way of Chuquisaca and Potosí. Draw this trip in orange. Label the cities of Corrientes, Santa Fé, and Chuquisaca red. (Your South American map should now be complete.)

✓ **Checking the Catechism**
Older students may read the *CCC*'s text paragraphs 849-856 (144, 150, 172-173, and 193) on the missionary mandate of the Church. Younger students may study Catholic Action in their catechisms.

 Searching Scripture
Read some of the "thrilling stories from the *Acts of the Apostles*" (page 142) in Acts 2:1-13 and Acts 10:44-49. Remember that God will not ask you to do anything without first providing the gifts and the grace to accomplish his task. Read Luke 12:11-12.

Chapter 14–In Which Father Francis' Rest in Trujillo Comes to an End

Vocabulary
with extraordinary *clarity*   *fast*
This was not mere *oratory*   *sanctity*

Comprehension Questions/Narration Prompts
1. Name three reasons why Francis was excited about going to Trujillo.
2. What did Father Francis believe to the prefect prayer for winning graces for every man, woman, and child?
3. What was Father Francis' new assignment in the middle of 1604?

Forming Opinions/Drawing Conclusions
1. "The spiritual life of Trujillo was by no means thriving. The people were careless . . ." (page 154). What does this mean? How would you describe the spiritual life of your own community?
2. What is the "grace of abandonment" (page 160)?

Growing in Holiness
1. The Commissary General, John Venido, writes to Father Francis, ". . . use your talents to the best possible advantage" (page 154). Ask others to help you establish a list of talents that you can use for the glory of God.
2. Father Francis speaks of "the value of time" (page 156). Assess how you currently use the "coin wherewith one purchases either Heaven or Hell" (page 154). Are you spending your time wisely?

✓ Checking the Catechism
Father Francis speaks on the perfection of God, "And those who would give themselves to Him without reserve would have taken a long stride towards sharing in that perfection" (page 160). Older students may read what the *CCC* teaches about the necessity of the faithful acquiring perfection in text paragraphs 825, 1709, 2013, and 2028 (428). Younger students may review the perfections of God in their own catechisms.

Searching Scripture
1. Francis is concerned about the "lukewarmness" (page 156) of the Trujillo citizens' spirituality. Read Revelation (Apocalypse) 3:14-16 about God's response to the lukewarm.
2. "The people of Trujillo were a stiff-necked, obstinate lot" (page 158). Read about the stiff-necked people of Moses' time in Exodus 32:9-10 and Deuteronomy 9:13.

Chapter 15 – In Which Father Francis Touches the Hearts of Lima's Citizens

 Vocabulary

Merchants *vied* with one another
fire and *brimstone*
sackcloth
expiation

 Comprehension Questions/Narration Prompts
1. According to Father Francis, what makes a man a good preacher?
2. What activity of Father Francis' surprised Brother Porter shortly before Christmas in 1604?
3. What effect did the sermon given by Francis have on the citizens of Lima?
4. Why did the Viceroy call Francis out of the monastery later that night?

 Forming Opinions/Drawing Conclusions
1. Explain the following expression from page 167, "the spirit of the world in plain evidence."
2. Explain the meaning of the word "concupiscence."
3. After his sermon in the streets of Lima in December 1604, Father Francis thanked God for allowing him to be His tool. What does this mean? How can you be a tool of God?

 For Further Study
Study the Seven Penitential Psalms as mentioned on page 174: Psalm 6, 32 (31), 38 (37), 51 (50), 102 (101), 130 (129), and 143 (142). Memorize at least one passage.

 Growing in Holiness
In imitation of St. Francis Solano, spend time every day on your knees "listening to what He has to tell [you]" (page 166). Strive "always to follow the promptings of the Holy Spirit" (page 166) that result from these meditations.

✓ **Checking the Catechism**
Older students can read text paragraphs 2585-89 and 2596-97 (243 and 540) in the *CCC* regarding the Psalms. If desired, complete Activity #67 in *100 Activities*. Younger students may review penance and mortification in their catechisms.

 Searching Scripture
1. "Unless you do penance, you shall all likewise perish" (pages 167-68). Read Luke 13: 2-3.
2. Read 1 John 2:15-17. ("For all that is in the world . . ." page 168)
3. Read Psalm 51 (50). ("Have mercy on me, O God . . ." page 171)
4. Read Psalm 130:1-4 (129:1-4a) which corresponds to the four quotations found on page 175.

Chapter 16–In Which Father Francis Reunites His Old Friend John with the Franciscan Family

★REVIEW★ Vocabulary

earnestly *entreated* him
failure as a religious always *rankled*

calumnies (calumny)
Third Order (tertiary)

??? Comprehension Questions/Narration Prompts
1. What effect did Father Francis' sermon have on the Royal Council?
2. Explain the effect that the "great sermon" had in terms of souls reunited in friendship with God. What proclamation did the Viceroy make regarding that night?
3. How does the devil interfere when we attempt to talk with God?
4. Why did John not want his son to be a priest?

 Forming Opinions/Drawing Conclusions
1. Explain the following sentence from page 179, "Twice, within a few hours' time, He had given a poor friar's words superhuman power."
2. Summarize Father Francis' view on the wise use of time for lay people.
3. Why does Father Francis use the words "Here we are" instead of the more traditional "Here I am" when praying to the heavenly Father? Explain why this phrase is so powerful.
4. Explore why "pride [is] the greatest weed in the garden of the soul" (page 187). Name several people in the Bible who lost their struggle with pride. Relate the consequences of their actions.

✝ Growing in Holiness
Begin to use St. Francis Solano's three words "Here we are" when praying. Use these words when you begin prayer or as a short prayer in itself throughout the day.

✓ Checking the Catechism
"How clearly Francis showed the dreadfulness of sin . . . venial sins . . . mortal sin . . ." (page 178). Older students may read the teachings on venial and mortal sin in the *CCC* in text paragraphs 1852-1864 (392-396) while younger students review these teachings in their own catechisms.

 Searching Scripture
1. Read these biblical passages regarding the destruction of the cities of Sodom and Gomorrah: Genesis 18:20-19:29, Jeremiah (Jeremias) 23:14, and Matthew 10:11-15.
2. "Here I am, Lord . . . even as the boy Samuel had done in the Old Testament" (page 183). Read the story of the Lord calling Samuel in 1 Samuel (1 Kings) 3:1-18.

Chapter 17–In Which Father Francis Preaches in the Streets of Lima and Instructs Brother John in the Ways of a Saint

Vocabulary
despite his many *lapses* from grace
these *excursions* from the cloister

Order of Penance
Order of Friars Minor

Comprehension Questions/Narration Prompts
1. What did John begin to understand about true happiness?
2. What happened on March 23, 1606?
3. What new appointment did Father Francis receive in the spring of 1606?
4. What is the familiar motto of the Franciscan Order?
5. According to Father Francis, what is the most wonderful book in the world?

Forming Opinions/Drawing Conclusions
1. "How Brother John loved mission stories!" (page 196) In your own words, tell about one of Father Francis' mission trips from a previous chapter.
2. Discuss the value of prayers and sacrifices that are offered for others.
3. What lessons did Brother John learn from Father Francis? Is there a holy person in your life with whom you can talk and learn?

Growing in Holiness
1. Father Francis tells Brother John that he has had an important role in converting others to the Christian faith—he has been a missionary by reciting prayers for the missionary friars, making sacrifices for them, offering up trials during his day, fighting back impatient words, and sharing with others. Become a missionary yourself by reciting an Our Father or Hail Mary every day for the missionaries in other countries. Make small sacrifices each day for them.
2. Spend time, as Francis did, before a crucifix. Sit; look at Jesus, and think of Calvary.

Searching Scripture
1. "That in the midst of great wealth he should suddenly glimpse the blessing of being poor in spirit" (page 190). Read the story of the rich young man in Matthew 19:16-30. Read too Psalm 49 (48): 6-21.
2. "Suddenly, almost miraculously, the scales were falling from his eyes . . ." (page 191). Read how the scales fell from St. Paul's eyes in Acts 9:1-19.
3. "Even a great criminal can save his soul in a few seconds" (page 192). Read how Jesus promised salvation to a criminal in Luke 23:33-43.

Chapter 18–In Which Father Francis Continues to Teach by Word and Example until the Moment of His Death

 Vocabulary

there was great *consternation*
he said *contritely*
Last Sacraments
Apostles' Creed

 Comprehension Questions/Narration Prompts
1. Father Francis predicted his own death months before it actually occurred. What date did he predict as the day of his return to God?
2. What did Father Francis feel was the best way to win souls for heaven?
3. What two titles of Father Francis are mentioned in this chapter?
4. What prayer did Father Francis request to hear as he was dying? What were his last words?

 Forming Opinions/Drawing Conclusions
1. What is Father Francis' view of suffering?
2. What lessons did Father Francis teach by word and example from his sickbed?
3. Explain the "one song" analogy that Father Francis used.

 For Further Study
Research the Gran Chaco, which has been called "the Green Hell." Into what three countries does this wild plain extend? About how many square miles are covered by the Gran Chaco? What two main rivers water this plain? When did Bolivia and Paraguay fight over the Gran Chaco? What natural resources are contained in this South American plain?

 Growing in Holiness
If you do not yet have the Apostles' Creed memorized, please memorize this important prayer now. Why did St. Francis Solano hold this prayer in such high regard?

 **Timeline Work**
Add the events from 1590 through 1675 to complete your timeline.

✓ **Checking the Catechism**
In the *CCC*, older students may study the profession of faith made in the creeds as well as the difference between the Nicene and Apostles' Creed by reading text paragraphs 185-197 (33-35). If desired, complete Activity #34 and/or Actitivy #74 in *100 Activities*. Younger students may review the Apostles' Creed in their own catechisms.

Saint Francis Solano

✎ Book Summary Test for *Saint Francis Solano*

Directions: Answer in complete sentences. If necessary, use the back page for additional writing space. (100 possible points, 20 points for each answer.)

1. What religious order did St. Francis choose to enter? At what age did he enter?

    _____
    _____

2. Name some of the towns in Spain where Francis served his order. What positions of authority did he have? What special talent did he possess that he used to serve God?

    _____
    _____
    _____

3. Where did St. Francis Solano wish to go to be a missionary? About how many years did he have to wait to become a missionary? Where was he sent to serve as a missionary?

    _____
    _____
    _____

4. By what titles was St. Francis Solano known? Explain why these are appropriate titles for him.

    _____
    _____

5. Name at least three holy habits you have learned from St. Francis Solano.

    _____
    _____
    _____
    _____

Saint Francis Solano, Wonder-Worker of the New World and Apostle of Argentina and Peru

Answer Key to Comprehension Questions

Chapter 1 – In Which We Meet Francis Solano, the Mayor's Son
1. The first reason Francis gave for wanting to become a Franciscan was that the poverty of the Franciscan Order appealed to him. Secondly, he was excited about the possibility of going to Africa as a missionary.
2. Francis' "important business" was to tell his parents of his decision to answer God's call to become a Franciscan priest.
3. Francis believed that the best way to fulfill God's Will is through obedience to one's superiors.

Chapter 2 – In Which Francis Receives the Habit and Counsels His Friend
1. Francis was required to delay his entrance into the religious life as his parents and teachers felt that he should complete the entire course of study offered at the Jesuit College in Montilla. This delayed his entrance into the priesthood by three years.
2. Father Peter believed that the grace of emptying our hearts in order to hold Jesus is given to *everyone*.
3. The Franciscan friars accepted Francis Solano as a novice in 1569 when he was twenty years old.

Chapter 3 – In Which Francis Tells Us His Secret to Holiness
1. On behalf of his friend John, Francis wished to offer prayers that John be given the special grace to come back as a priest to the Franciscan Order.
2. The Father Guardian stated that the "best coin with which to ransom sinners" is a love of suffering and hardship.
3. Due to overcrowding in the friary of Seville, Francis' new cell was located in the bell tower of the church where a crude shelter was constructed for him.
4. Francis believed that the "best prayer that a human being can offer" is to offer ". . . himself and his actions to the Eternal Father in union with Christ's death upon Calvary—particularly at Holy Mass" (page 26).

Chapter 4 – In Which Father Francis Continues to Glorify God in His Work
1. The Father Guardian gave Francis the job of choir director in the year 1576.
2. According to Father Francis, all that matters is that God be glorified and served.
3. The death of Francis' father and the poor health of his mother prompted Father Francis' return to the friary in Montilla. His assignment there, as at Loreto, was to train the community in singing.
4. The younger friars at the friary in Montilla felt that if Francis had continued to live in the world, his name would have been famous due to his musical abilities.

Chapter 5 – In Which Father Francis Teaches His Novices Valuable Lessons
1. After applying for a transfer from Montilla, Father Francis was sent to Arizafa in the province of Castile. His new position there was that of Novice Master.
2. Father Francis used the analogy of a rosebush to teach his novices about growing in the service of God.
3. Father Francis acquired the additional job of preaching to the townspeople of Montoro when the novitiate was transferred to San Francisco del Monte. Two years later, he was elected to the position of Father Guardian of the monastery.

Chapter 6 – In Which Father Francis Endangers His Life to Fight the Plague
1. In an attempt to stem the progress of the plague, the citizens of Montoro burned every house where the plague had struck.
2. In order to fight the plague more effectively, Father Francis organized the townspeople by praying with them, dividing the labor, establishing a hospital for the ill in a farmhouse out of town, and insuring that those who had died were buried promptly.

Chapter 7 – In Which Francis Becomes a Missionary at Last
1. By his courageous actions during the plague, Father Bonaventure proved that "the most ordinary people can become holy in a short time if only they will give themselves completely to the Heavenly Father to do with as He wills" (page 66).
2. Francis wanted to leave his post in Montoro to "escape the honors now being heaped upon him for his heroism during the plague" (page 68).
3. After five years in Granada, Francis was given a new assignment—he was to accompany the Franciscan Father Balthazar Navarro to Tucumán in the northern region of Argentina.
4. Several conditions or circumstances made the job of the missionaries in South America difficult including the tradition of pagan rites, the lack of transportation across the many miles of Argentine wilderness, the poor Christian example of some of the Spanish colonists, and the numerous dialects spoken by the natives.

Chapter 8 – In Which Father Francis Saves Many Souls at Sea
1. As he began his missionary career, Father Francis' first students were the slaves that were being transported in the hold of the ship so that they could be sold in the market in Lima, Peru. Father Francis obtained permission from the captain to give instruction in the Faith to these passengers.
2. A dreadful storm arose in the Gulf of Gorgona and threw the ship upon a reef; as the ship was in danger of sinking immediately, Father Francis and his companions baptized and gave general absolution to all on board who wished the sacraments. Hundreds of souls were baptized that day.
3. In an attempt to add force to his prayers to stop the storm at sea, Francis began to scourge himself.
4. Francis alerted the men on shore and let them know that men were still alive on board the half-ship by lighting a box of altar candles that he had found floating in the sea.

Chapter 9 – In Which Father Francis and His Companions Are Stranded
1. As he was swimming toward the rescue boat, Father Francis took off his habit so that he could swim better. He accidentally threw his bundled habit into the water where it sank out of sight. (He later recovered his habit along the shore where he and his companions were stranded.)
2. Father Balthazar took the rescue boat with several men and started the dangerous journey to Panama to get help.
3. After Father Balthazar left, Father Francis distracted the sailors by having them build a shelter for a small statue of our Lady that had been saved from the ship.

Chapter 10 – In Which Francis and His Companions Arrive in Lima
1. The men who disobeyed the order that all food must be blessed by Father Francis before it was eaten died shortly after they ate the food.
2. Father Francis and his companions traveled along the shore as they began their 600-mile walk from Payta to Lima, as this region was almost a desert; their main source of food would be fish.
3. Father Francis and his companions hoped to meet Archbishop Turibius in Lima; however, he was 300 miles away administering the Sacrament of Confirmation. Francis, however, did meet his old friend John from the friary at Mantilla.

Chapter 11 – In Which Father Francis Learns about the Indians of Socotonio
1. John told his old friend Father Francis that he no longer desired to be a priest; he liked fine clothes, felt obedience to a superior would be difficult and restrictive, and liked to invest his money and watch it grow. He was now married and had become very worldly.
2. The governor, Don Andres, was amazed at Father Francis' ability to learn the native languages and dialects. Father Francis humbly attributed this ability to Don Andres' tutoring as well as to the intercession of St. Bonaventure.
3. Father Francis explains to Don Andres that St. Bonaventure is the Franciscan patron saint of students just as St. Thomas Aquinas is the Dominican patron saint of students. (Remember to ask both of these saints for their help the next time you need to do some difficult schoolwork!)

Chapter 12 – In Which Father Francis Makes Friends with the Pagan Tribes
1. The stick that Father Francis obtained from Father John was used to find a spring to provide water for the Socotonio tribe.
2. Besides providing valuable water, the new spring also allowed two mills to be built so that the inhabitants of Socotonio could use waterpower to grind grain such as wheat.
3. Francis became known as the "Apostle of Tucumán" due to his work in the city of Tucumán as well as his labors in the mission field within the district of Tucumán.
4. In 1595, Father Francis was appointed *Custos* of all the Tucumán missions.
5. When Father Francis met the fierce pagan tribe led by Peter Cotero, he took his violin and a crucifix as "weapons."
6. In His infinite mercy, God gave Father Francis "the gift of understanding, and of being understood in, all the Indian dialects" (page 135) so that he might be an effective missionary.

Chapter 13 – In Which Father Francis Converts a Great Many Souls
1. Father Francis converted around nine thousand South American tribal members on that blessed Holy Thursday.
2. Father Francis claimed that suffering—freely embraced for love of souls—is the secret of the Christian life.
3. In this chapter, Father Francis, *Custos* of Tucumán, was appointed Vicar of the friary of St. Mary of the Angels in Lima. He then became the Father Guardian of this monastery. However, several months later, he was relieved of the responsibility of this position and assigned as a simple friar in Trujillo.

Chapter 14 – In Which Father Francis' Rest in Trujillo Comes to an End
1. Francis was excited about going to Trujillo as he would be near the beautiful ruins of Chan Chan, he would be a simple friar with little responsibility and authority, and he would be another three hundred miles from Tucumán where his reputation as a successful missionary was well known.
2. Father Francis believed that the perfect prayer for winning graces for every man, woman, and child is the Holy Sacrifice of the Mass.
3. In the middle of 1604, Father Francis was reassigned to his former position of Father Guardian of St. Mary of the Angels monastery in Lima.

Chapter 15 – In Which Father Francis Touches the Hearts of Lima's Citizens
1. Father Francis believed that "To preach well, a man must have something to say—something he has learned in prayer" (page 166).
2. Shortly before Christmas in 1604, Father Francis' told Brother Porter that he was going out. This surprised Brother Porter as Father Francis rarely left the friary, especially during the evening hours.
3. Father Francis' sermon had a tremendous effect on the citizens of Lima. Many of them wished to receive the Sacrament of Penance, donned sackcloth, and expressed a fear that the city of Lima was to be destroyed by an earthquake. They processed through the streets with

the Blessed Sacrament, recited the Penitential Psalms, and performed public penance for their sins. The city was in a near panic.
4. The Viceroy called Father Francis out of the monastery later that night in order to have him clarify the text of the sermon he had made to Lima's citizens.

Chapter 16 – In Which Father Francis Reunites His Old Friend John with the Franciscan Family
1. The effect that Father Francis' sermon had on the Royal Council was the same effect it had had on the citizens of Lima. The members of the Royal Council feared for their spiritual and temporal well-being and were anxious to receive the Sacrament of Penance.
2. In terms of souls reunited in friendship with God, the "great sermon" caused eight thousand souls to become reconciled with God through Confession. Three thousand marriages were rectified, and countless children baptized. People made restitution, debts were paid, and stolen goods were returned. That night the Viceroy made a proclamation that "Surely this night will go down in history—and Father Francis' name with it!" (page 180).
3. When we attempt to talk with God, the devil often interferes by sending us distractions, causing us to be tired, and disturbing us "in a hundred irritating ways" (page 182).
4. John wanted his son to be like himself, interested in worldly success. John stubbornly believed that his son was needed at home and could not be spared from home to lead a religious life.

Chapter 17 – In Which Father Francis Preaches in the Streets of Lima and Instructs Brother John in the Ways of a Saint
1. John began to understand that true happiness consists in being rooted in God, in having faith in him instead of in creatures and things.
2. Archbishop Turibius Alphonsus de Mogrovejo, the second bishop of Lima, died on March 23, 1606.
3. In the spring of 1606, Father Francis was relieved of his duties as superior at St. Mary of the Angels Monastery. He was transferred to Lima's larger, less strict friary of San Francisco as a simple friar with no other responsibilities.
4. The familiar motto of the Franciscan Order that Father Francis spoke so joyfully was "God be praised!"
5. Father Francis believed that the most wonderful book in the world is the crucifix. (St. Thomas Aquinas also held this belief.)

Chapter 18 – In Which Father Francis Continues to Teach by Word and Example until the Moment of His Death
1. Father Francis accurately predicted that his death would occur on July 14, 1610.
2. Father Francis believed that the best way to win souls for heaven was through suffering.
3. St. Francis Solano is referred to as the "Apostle of Tucumán" and the "Apostle of Peru" in this chapter.
4. As he was dying, Father Francis requested to hear the Apostles' Creed. His last words were the Franciscan motto, "God be praised!"

Answer Key to Book Summary Test

1. St. Francis Solano chose to become an Alcantrine Franciscan priest. He entered the friary at Montilla, Spain, in 1569 at the age of twenty and was ordained a priest in 1576.
2. St. Francis Solano served his order in Spain in the towns of Seville and Montilla as a choir director, in Arizafa as Novice Master, in Montoro as Novice Master and Father Guardian (where he fought the plague), and as a priest and preacher in Granada. St. Francis was very gifted musically. He could sing well and played the violin.

Saint Francis Solano

3. For many years, St. Francis Solano earnestly desired to go to Africa to be a missionary and perhaps a martyr. In 1589, after waiting patiently and obediently for almost fifteen years, St. Francis Solano was assigned as a Franciscan missionary to South America.
4. St. Francis Solano is known as the "Apostle of Tucumán" due to the thousands of souls he converted to Christianity in this vast South American district. He has also been given the title of "Apostle of Peru" for all he accomplished there for God's kingdom. (St. Francis Solano is also commonly given the titles of "Thaumaturgus of the New World" and "Wonder Worker of the New World." (Thaumaturgus is a title given to select saints who are outstanding in their performance of miracles either during their lifetime or after their death.)
5. Answers will vary.

Study Guide for

Pauline Jaricot, Foundress of the Living Rosary and the Society for the Propagation of the Faith

Pauline Jaricot

Born to wealthy parents in Lyons of France.
Pauline loved her wardrobe, to party and dance.
A fall made her ill;
She sought out God's will.
Her eyes turned to heaven instead of romance.

Though most thought her crazy—thought she was mad,
Gave up her fine clothing—this was not a fad.
Vanity was fought;
Suffering it brought.
As she persevered, to her joy God did add.

Raised cash for the missions, success she did know.
So much success that her enemies did grow.
So she stepped aside,
Taking all in stride,
Stayed true to her God, growth in virtue did show.

A living rosary, this group too she formed,
Good reading, prayers for France—that sinners be reformed.
Alms, good works, and prayer,
Enemies to bear,
She endured and persevered, to God's will conformed.

A Christian model town was Pauline's big dream.
The agent she used had another scheme.
Debt was the result.
Though not Pauline's fault,
Spent all of her life the debt to redeem.

Trials, humiliations, scandal, tests of pride,
Her faith strong throughout all—God was her guide.
Not for her own fame,
Always for His name.
Pauline worked only that God be glorified.

Think what you can learn from this saint and her tale.
How you can apply it to help you prevail.
Then mold what you do
And boldly pursue
Her pattern of holiness. Follow her trail.

Timeline of Events

Year	Event
1776-83	American Revolutionary War fought
1789	French Revolution begins (to 1799); John Carroll named bishop of Baltimore
1799	Pauline Marie Jaricot born on July 22nd in Lyons, France; Napoleon Bonaparte comes to power in France
1803	President Jefferson secures the Louisiana Purchase for the United States
1809	Napoleon Bonaparte takes possession of the Papal States (until 1815); St. Elizabeth Seton establishes Sisters of Charity in Emmitsburg, Maryland
1812	Pauline receives her First Holy Communion
1814	Pauline falls and becomes seriously ill; death of Pauline's mother
1815	Paul Jaricot, Pauline's brother, marries Julie Germain; Battle of Waterloo; French monarchy re-established
1816	Pauline hears life-changing sermon of Father Wendel Wurtz; meets Father John Vianney for the first time; and takes vow of perpetual virginity on Christmas Day
1819	Pauline begins collection from "repartees" in spring
1822	On May 3rd, the Association for the Propagation of the Faith reorganizes. (By 1910, this society had collected more than $78 million.)
1823	Pope Pius VII gives his blessing to the Society for the Propagation of the Faith; Pauline's brother Phileas is ordained to the priesthood
1826	Pauline begins devotion of Living Rosary on December 8th
1829-30	Pauline's sister Laurette and brother Phileas die; revolution in France
1832	Living Rosary given formal approval by Pope Gregory XVI; Pauline purchases home "Loreto" on hillside outside of Lyons, France
1834	Civil strife in Lyons; Pauline's father dies; Pauline becomes seriously ill
1835	Pauline stays with Madeleine Sophie Barat in Rome. Her heart condition is miraculously cured in Mugnano—attributed to the intercession of St. Philomena; Pauline remains in Rome for nine months, until May 1836
1837	Philomena declared a saint in January—feast day set for August 11; erection of a chapel in Ars dedicated to St. Philomena
1838	One million members belong to the Association of the Living Rosary
1841	St. John Bosco ordained a priest
1845	Pauline purchases factory of Rustrel; conversion of John Henry Newman
1846	Apparition at La Salette, France; Pauline struggles with bankruptcy
1850	Pauline is rejected as foundress of the Propagation of the Faith Society
1852	Opening of "St. Philomena's Path" on December 8th at Loreto
1858	Apparition in Lourdes, France, of Our Lady to Bernadette Soubirous
1859	Death of John Vianney in August
1861	Beginning of the United States Civil War (until 1865)
1862	Pauline Jaricot dies in Lyons, France, on January 9th after studying and practicing Louis de Montfort's *True Devotion to the Blessed Virgin Mary*
1869-70	First Vatican Council meets
1919	Pauline Jaricot recognized as foundress for Society of the Propagation of the Faith; in 1930 her cause for beatification was begun; Pauline was declared venerable on January 9, 1963

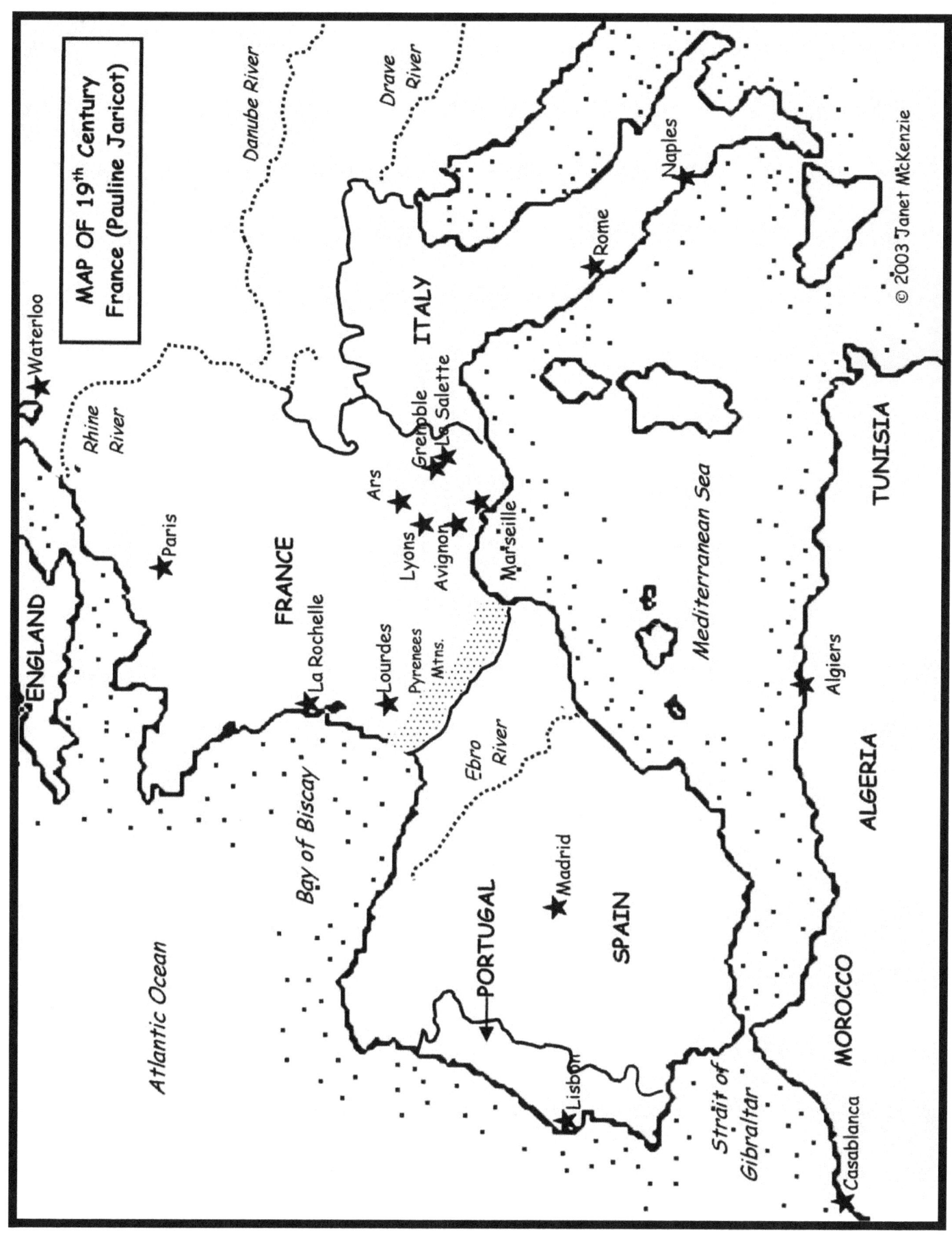

Chapters 1 through 4—In Which Young Pauline Suffers, Recovers from Her Accident, and Tries to Find God's Plan for Her Life

 Vocabulary

dressmaker and *milliner*
Pauline was "*bled*"
large *leghorn* hat
simple sermon on *vanity*

High Mass
Introit
Epiphany
director

Comprehension Questions/Narration Prompts

Chapter 1
1. What year was Pauline Jaricot born? In what country did she live?
2. What were Pauline's main interests when she was fourteen and fifteen years old?

Chapter 2
1. Due to her poor health, Pauline was not told about two major family events. Name these events.
2. What was the "drastic change" that occurred in Chapter 2?

Chapter 3
1. What occurred to cause a positive change in Pauline's condition?
2. Pauline had a "nagging fear" (page 17) that God had a special plan for her since the priest mentioned the possibility at her confession. Why did Pauline feel that her vocation was not to be a nun?
3. What did Pauline hope Father John Wurtz would do for her?

Chapter 4
1. What was the Jaricot family's reaction to Pauline's new lifestyle?
2. Why was Pauline making sacrifices such as giving up her lovely clothes and caring for sick people whom she found repulsive? What new sacrifice did she decide to make to "speed up" God's revelation to her?

 Forming Opinions/Drawing Conclusions

1. Was it wrong of Pauline to accept a ring from Lucien? When is it appropriate and necessary to have a secret? When is it not?
2. Is it a good idea to try to change people after marriage? Explain your answer.
3. Pauline told her father that he had always given her everything she wanted, but he gave her too much. "It's kept me from hearing God's voice" (page 20). Discuss how material things can block out God.

For Further Study

The story of Pauline begins in the year 1814 shortly before her fifteenth birthday. Her father has a prospering business and has not been "condemned to the poverty that had been the lot of so many in France since the Revolution twenty-five year before" (page 1). Research the French Revolution, which began in 1789. Include the following in your research: "Liberty, Equality, Fraternity"; the Battle of Bastille; Lafayette; The Declaration of the Rights of Man; Louis XVI; Marie Antoinette; the Civil Constitution of the Clergy; Maximilien Robespierre; the Reign of Terror; and Napoleon Bonaparte.

 Growing in Holiness

In these four chapters, Pauline is searching for happiness. We all want to be happy. St. Augustine stated in his *Confessions*, "Our heart is restless until it rests in You." The happiness of this life is temporary and incomplete. Take stock of your life. Are you restless and not quite happy? What can you do to connect to the Source of all happiness? As Pauline did at the beginning of her search, receive the Sacrament of Penance.

 Timeline Work

Taping sheets of plain paper end-to-end, make a timeline representing the years from 1776 through 1919. Let three inches equal 25 years. Mark on your timeline the dates and events from 1776 through 1816, using information from page 56 of this study guide.

 Checking the Catechism

"'Dear Lord, do with me anything You wish, but spare my child that cross!' begged Madame Jaricot from her sickbed. 'Take my life. . . . *anything* . . . only let Pauline recover'" (pages 10-11). Older students may read about Christ's suffering upon the cross for us in text paragraphs 599-623 (117-124) of the *Catechism of the Catholic Church*. If desired, complete Activity #6 in *100 Activities Based on the Catechism of the Catholic Church* (*100 Activities*). Younger students may study Christ's Passion and Death in their own catechisms.

 Searching Scripture

". . . God is not only a God of justice but a God of mercy, too" (page 14). Read what the Bible says about God as a God of justice in Isaiah (Isaias) 11:3-5, Jeremiah (Jeremias) 23:5-6, and Psalm 72 (71):1-4. Read too what it has to say about a God of mercy: Psalm 136 (135), Sirach 51:29 (Ecclesiasticus 51:37), Luke 6:36, and Titus 3:4-7.

Chapters 5 through 7—In Which Pauline Begins Her Mission despite All Obstacles

 Vocabulary

a *counsel* of Saint Francis de Sales
unpretentious a movement
sensed the *pathos*
repose of her soul

foreign missions
converts
catechist
Eminence

 Comprehension Questions/Narration Prompts

Chapter 5
1. What new area of work did Pauline decide to take on? What was the reaction to this new idea of Pauline's?
2. Why did Anthony Jaricot think both Pauline and Phileas were "different"?
3. What did Anthony Jaricot decide to do to ease his mind?

Chapter 6
1. Name some of Pauline's accomplishments at the factory?
2. What did Pauline organize for the foreign missions?
3. What was the reaction of the members of the Reparatrices of the Heart of Jesus to Phileas's announcement of his decision to study for the priesthood?
4. What counsel did Father Wurtz give to Pauline regarding her spiritual practices?

Chapter 7
1. How did Anthony Jaricot react to the "new" Pauline?
2. What was Pauline's new inspiration to insure the collection of the "penny per week"? Whose approval did she seek before she implemented this new plan?

 Forming Opinions/Drawing Conclusions
1. To whom was Pauline speaking on page 24?
2. What did Phileas mean when he stated that the Protestants are "anxious to spread error" (page 34)? What is the "truth" he spoke of?
3. How has Pauline's life and outlook changed in the past four years?
4. What would you do if you were Pauline when she was confronted by the priest who was critical of her collecting so much money for the Society for the Propagation of the Faith? List several possible solutions.

For Further Study
Pauline and the Society for the Propagation of the Faith raised money to send to the foreign missions, especially in China. Research the current status of Christian missionaries

in China. What percentage of the population of China today is Christian? Does freedom of religion exist there today?

 Growing in Holiness

Notice the effect Pauline had on the behavior and attitude of her brother Phileas. "Suddenly he seemed to have tired of being a rich man's son, with nothing to do but amuse himself. He had now taken to hearing Mass daily, reading spiritual books, visiting the sick poor and those in prison, and dispensing alms with a generous hand. 'The spirit must be catching' was the general verdict'" (pages 29-30). Choose to imitate either Phileas in his spiritual conversion (attend Mass more frequently, spend time each day in spiritual reading, visit the sick or imprisoned, give alms to those in need) or Pauline in beginning a fundraising mission for a person or group in need. Remember that people may be more affected by observing your actions than listening to your words. Take to heart the words of St. Francis of Assisi, "Tell everyone around you of the great love of God. When necessary, use words."

Geography

Trace the map on page 57 of this study guide. Label and color these seas and oceans blue: Atlantic, Bay of Bisque, Strait of Gibraltar, and Mediterranean as well as these rivers: Rhine, Danube, Ebro, and Drave. Label the Pyrenees Mountains and color them brown. (The remaining map will be completed in Chapters 21-24.)

✓ Checking the Catechism

On page 34, Pauline considered the doctrine of the Mystical Body of Christ. Re-read the third full paragraph on this page. Then read the corresponding text paragraphs in the *Catechism of the Catholic Church* on the Mystical Body of Christ: 787-796 (156-158) and on the treasury of the Church: 1476-77 (312). Read what St. Paul says in his famous dissertation on the Mystical Body of Christ in 1 Corinthians 12:12-27.

📖 Searching Scripture

"Gone were the days when she had tried to sell herself by being the center of attraction in her own little circle. Approval, admiration, the friendship of others, were still heart-warming things, of course, but she could live without them" (page 27). Read the following Biblical passages on this topic: Proverbs 3:34, Matthew 6:1-4, Matthew 6:16-18, and Matthew 19:30.

Chapters 8 through 10—In Which Pauline Is Beset by Obstacles and Begins the Association of the Living Rosary

 Vocabulary

jealous and *malicious* gossip
alarmed by her *pallor*
a dangerous *presumption*
overcome with *remorse*

pastor
Monsignor
laity
clergy

Comprehension Questions/Narration Prompts

Chapter 8
1. Why did Monsignor Gourdiat believe that Pauline would be starting to have trouble regarding her mission work? What caution does he give her?
2. What were some of the unkind comments made about Pauline as she continued her work for the missions?
3. How did Pauline spend her days?
4. What made Pauline and Victor uneasy about helping the Church in America?

Chapter 9
1. What compromise was reached that allowed funds to also be given to the American missions?
2. In September 1822, the Society of the Propagation of the Faith was divided into two central offices. Where were they? What were the good works required for members of the society?
3. Were Pauline's suspicions about Father Inglesi well founded?

Chapter 10
1. What did Pauline's spiritual director advise her to do?
2. Pauline came down hard on herself, declaring, "I'm a selfish, good-for-nothing wretch" (page 62). What did she see as her solution? Did Father Wurtz approve? Explain.
3. What was Pauline's new work to be?

 Forming Opinions/Drawing Conclusions
1. ". . . hundreds of people are becoming mission-minded" (page 47). What does it mean to be "mission-minded"? What can you do to become more mission-minded and help others to do the same?
2. "Suffering always accompanies any worthwhile work. The sooner you learn that, and—relying upon God's Providence—accept it cheerfully, the better off you'll be" (page 47). In what ways is Pauline suffering for her work? What ways can you offer to suffer for the work of the Church?

3. "After all, hadn't her own great patron, St. Paul the Apostle, cautioned against women taking too prominent a part in Church affairs" (page 48)? Read 1 Corinthians 14:34-35, Titus 2:3-5, and 1 Peter 3:1-6. What did St. Paul believe regarding the role of women in the Church and in marriage?

 For Further Study

Research the Society for the Propagation of the Faith in the United States online at www.propfaith.org. Begin to pray daily for the Church's missionary work as recommended by the Society for the Propagation of the Faith: one Our Father, one Hail Mary, one Glory Be, and the two ejaculations, "St. Francis Xavier, pray for us" and "St. Thérèse of Lisieux, pray for us." (See page 56 for Pauline's original membership requirements.) Give generously on World Mission Sunday on the next-to-last Sunday of October—the annual Society for the Propagation of the Faith's world-wide collection.

 Growing in Holiness

1. The foreign missions and the return to the Faith of France's working-class people were Pauline's two major priorities. "For these two intentions, she and her Reparatrices continued to make the Way of the Cross each day and to visit the Blessed Sacrament as frequently as possible" (page 50). Begin to pray and sacrifice daily for our country.
2. "The future of France is in the hands of youngsters. . . . If we encourage them to read about God and His saints now, it may change the history of our country" (page 65). "Pope Leo the Twelfth had recently urged all loyal Catholics to promote the cause of good reading" (page 65). "An Association of Prayer is what we need. . . . That, added to the good reading, could work wonders. Especially if the prayer had some thought behind it, like meditation on the mysteries of the rosary" (page 66). How can you implement these spiritual maxims into your own daily life?

✓ **Checking the Catechism**

"It was surely a lost country. Never had there been such a godless place. People cared only about making money. Pleasure, ease, worldly power—these were the things that interested them. Certainly one day God would severely punish such spiritual blindness" (page 62). Read the *Catechism of the Catholic Church* text paragraphs 2534-57 (531-533) on the tenth commandment, especially paragraphs 2545 and 2548.

 Searching Scripture

Read Matthew 6:19-34, Luke 6:20, Luke 14:33, and James 5:1-5—all continuations of the theme of the attachment to worldly goods.

Chapters 11 through 15—In Which Both Pauline's Sister and Brother Die, and She Herself Becomes Seriously Ill

 Vocabulary

wrote a *circular* letter
was cured of *sciatica*
smaller *conflagrations*
wouldn't be *prudent*

contemplate
Albigensian heresy
Ursuline
Papal Nuncio

 Comprehension Questions/Narration Prompts

Chapter 11
1. What were the aims of the Living Rosary?
2. What were the objections to the rosary that Pauline encountered?
3. How did Pauline counter these objections?

Chapter 12
1. Who was poisoned at the Hotel-Dieu Hospital in Lyons and why?
2. How did Pauline's brother Phileas die?

Chapter 13
1. Why did Pauline purchase the house she later named "Loreto"?
2. How did Pauline become acquainted with Philomena?

Chapter 14
1. Why in 1834 were Pauline and her friends at Loreto forced to take refuge for several days in a nearby cave?
2. Why did they feel protected and safe?

Chapter 15
1. How many people died in the worker uprising in Lyons in 1834?
2. Why did Pauline wish to go to Mugnano, near Naples, and Rome in the spring of 1835? How far was this journey to be?

Forming Opinions/Drawing Conclusions
1. Why has the rosary always been a special concern of the Dominican order?
2. ". . . to contemplate and to give to others the fruit of one's contemplation" (page 68). What two obligations does this Dominican motto place upon its members?
3. "Lord, please accept me as a victim" (page 89). What does it mean to offer oneself as a victim soul? (Re-read the bottom of page 62.) What does this enable you to predict about Pauline's life?

For Further Study

Do some background research into the Industrial Revolution which lasted from around 1760 to 1790. Where did this "revolution" begin and why? Why was it not really a revolution at all? Study the Revolution of 1830 and the Revolution of 1848. What were the results of these two revolutions and how were they, as well as the uprising in Lyons in 1834, connected to the Industrial Revolution?

 Growing in Holiness

1. Ms. Windeatt uses several titles to refer to the Blessed Virgin in Chapter 11 of *Pauline Jaricot:* Mirror of Justice, Queen of all Saints, and Our Lady of the Rosary. All three of these titles are also used in the Litany of Loreto, which is also known as the Litany of the Blessed Virgin. Recite this litany for the same intention as Pauline offered herself—"the cause of peace—and for the poor" (page 89).
2. Additionally, you may wish to join the Association of the Living Rosary. Remember that in doing so you are committing yourself to the recitation of one decade of the rosary (one Our Father, ten Hail Marys, and meditation on the mystery that will be assigned to you) any hour of the day or night daily until death for the intention of the triumph of the Immaculate Heart of Mary and the honor of St. Philomena. A voluntary donation of $12.00 per year is suggested to meet the expenses of the Apostolate. To join, write to: The Living Rosary, P.O. Box 1303, Dickinson, TX 77539. If you write to enroll someone other than yourself, you need that person's permission. Be certain he/she is aware of the commitment. For more information on the Living Rosary Association, go to www.philomena.org.

 Timeline Work

Add the dates and events from 1819 through 1834 to your timeline.

✓ **Checking the Catechism**

Older students may also read corresponding text paragraphs in the *Catechism of the Catholic Church*: 971, 1674, 2673-2679, and 2708 (96-100, 142, 196-199, 240, 546, and 562-563) on devotion to the Blessed Virgin Mary. Younger students may study this same topic in their own catechisms. If desired, complete Activity #71, "Sing of Mary," in *100 Activities*.

📖 **Searching Scripture**

Read what Holy Scripture has to say about labor and the laborer: Deuteronomy 24:15, Proverbs 6:6-11, Proverbs 10:4, Proverbs 14:23, Ecclesiastes 9:10, Malachi (Malachias) 3:5, Matthew 11:28, Luke 10:7, and 1 Thessalonians 5:12-13.

Chapters 16 through 20—In Which Pauline Is Cured of Her Heart Condition by the Intercession of St. Philomena

Vocabulary
gaily decked with *garlands*
was no *delusion*
was not a *myth*
in the *limelight*

Benediction
cause
abbots
Capuchin

Comprehension Questions/Narration Prompts

Chapter 16
1. List at least three good works performed by Pauline that are mentioned in this chapter.
2. What agreement did Pope Gregory XVI make with Pauline when they met at Madeleine Sophie Barat's convent in Rome in the summer of 1835?
3. What did the townspeople demand when Pauline arrived at Philomena's shrine in Mugnano?

Chapter 17
1. How did Pauline feel when she was about to die during the Benediction service at Philomena's shrine?
2. "Philomena *has* worked a miracle!" (page 102) What miracle occurred through the intercession of Philomena?

Chapter 18
1. What did Pauline do in Mugnano out of gratitude to Philomena?
2. What did the Papal Nuncio at Naples predict to Pauline about her future?
3. What did the pope give Pauline permission to do when she returned to Rome after her cure? What promise of his own did he vow that he would fulfill to Pauline?

Chapter 19
1. What happened in Rome that allowed the members of the Living Rosary to claim St. Dominic as a special friend and protector?
2. Why was Pauline's friend Marie uneasy about the Association of the Living Rosary taking St. Dominic as a patron?

Chapter 20
1. What gift had Pauline sent to Father John Vianney while she was in Italy?
2. To whose intercession did Father Vianney attribute the cures and conversions that were taking place in Ars?
3. When was St. Philomena canonized and what day is her feast celebrated in the Church?

Forming Opinions/Drawing Conclusions

1. How might you have felt in Pauline's place when the parish priest of Mugnano insisted that she take a triumphal march around the town after her cure?
2. What would it be like to be in the presence of a truly holy person such as Father John Vianney? Have you ever had this experience? Can you name someone you know who would fit into this category?

For Further Study

Research the Blood of Januarius—a miracle of the Eucharist. St. Januarius was a bishop during the persecution of Diocletian (late third and early fourth centuries). His relics are kept in the Cathedral of Naples. When does the solidified blood liquefy?

Growing in Holiness

Invoke the powerful intercession of St. Philomena by reciting her litany as composed by St. John Vianney. Note that this litany is for private recital only.

Lord have mercy on us. *Christ have mercy on us.* Lord have mercy on us. God the Father of Heaven, *have mercy on us.* God the Son, Redeemer of the world, *have mercy on us.* God the Holy Ghost, *have mercy on us.* Holy Trinity one God, *have mercy on us.* Holy Mary, Queen of Virgins, *have mercy on us.* St. Philomena, *pray for us* [recite *pray for us* at each asterisk]. St. Philomena, filled with the most abundant graces from thy very birth, *. St. Philomena, faithful imitator of Mary, *. St. Philomena, model of Virgins, *. St. Philomena, temple of the most perfect humility, *. St. Philomena, inflamed with zeal for the Glory of God, *. St. Philomena, victim of the love of Jesus, *. St. Philomena, example of strength and perseverance, *. St. Philomena, invincible champion of chastity, *. St. Philomena, mirror of the most heroic virtues, *. St. Philomena, firm and intrepid in the face of torments, *. St. Philomena, scourged like thy Divine Spouse, *. St. Philomena, pierced by a shower of arrows, *. St. Philomena, consoled by the Mother of God when in chains, *. St. Philomena, cured miraculously in prison, *. St. Philomena, comforted by Angels in thy torments, *. St. Philomena, who preferred torments and death to the splendors of a throne, *. St. Philomena, who converted the witnesses of thy Martyrdom, *. St. Philomena, who wore out the fury of thy executioners, *. St. Philomena, protectress of the innocent, *. St. Philomena, patron of youth, *. St. Philomena, refuge of the unfortunate, *. St. Philomena, health of the sick and the weak, *. St. Philomena, new light of the Church Militant, *. St. Philomena, who confounds the impiety of the world, *. St. Philomena, who stimulates the faith and courage of the faithful, *. St. Philomena, whose name is glorified in Heaven and feared in Hell, *. St. Philomena, made illustrious by the most striking miracles, *. St. Philomena, all powerful with God, *. St. Philomena, who reigns in glory, *. Lamb of God, Who takes away the sins of the world, *spare us, O Lord.* Lamb of God, Who takes away the sins of the world, *graciously hear us, O Lord*. Lamb of God, Who takes away the sins of the world, *have mercy on us.* V. Pray for us, great St. Philomena, R. *That we may be made worthy of the promises of Christ.* Let us pray. We implore Thee, O Lord, by the intercession of St. Philomena, Virgin and Martyr, who was ever most pleasing to Thy eyes by reason of her eminent purity and the practice of all the virtues, pardon us our sins and grant us all the graces we need [request here a special grace]. Amen.

Chapters 21 through 24—In Which Pauline Outlines the Plan for the Holy Childhood Association and Moves Forward in Her Plans to Develop a Model Christian Town

 Vocabulary

antagonism of Paul Jaricot
in *pensive* silence
furnish *bail* for himself
in *dubious* silence

almsgiving
Purgatory
sacrilege
shrine

 Comprehension Questions/Narration Prompts

Chapter 21
1. Marie Melquiond stated that Pauline had enemies. What did she believe caused many people to dislike or be envious of Pauline?
2. What was Pauline's new plan to save the abandoned children in China? What was this new organization to be called?

Chapter 22
1. What was the "Bank of Heaven" as instituted by Pauline Jaricot?
2. What level of support and encouragement did Pauline receive from her family?
3. What were Paul's misgivings about Pauline's trust of John Allioud?

Chapter 23
1. What did Pauline suggest to John in an effort to cheer him?
2. What kindness did Pauline offer to help John's friend Gustave Perre?

Chapter 24
What factors caused the women of Loreto to be less enthusiastic about Gustave than Pauline was?

Forming Opinions/Drawing Conclusions

1. How might Pauline's idea of a model Christian town work today in the United States? Have you ever wanted to be surrounded by other Catholic families all working together for a common goal? What might the advantages and problems of such a town be?
2. Gustave mentions an old Catholic custom, that of making three wishes when a visit is made to a Catholic church for the first time. What precautions are necessary to ensure that this custom is not practiced in a superstitious manner?

For Further Study

Check out the Holy Childhood Association—a society established in France in 1843 with the same principles as the Society for the Propagation of the Faith but for children. Bishop Charles de Forbin-Janson established this organization in 1843 following his consultation with Pauline Jaricot. Browse the American Internet site for the Holy Childhood Association at www.HolyChildhoodUSA.org. Perhaps you'd like to join!

 Growing in Holiness

Pauline stated, "It's a real privilege to be asked for prayers" (page 121), and "We'd all be better off if we'd only ask more people for prayers" (page 122). Begin the habit of asking others to remember you in prayer and of volunteering to pray for others. One Hail Mary well said is very powerful. As more people begin to request your prayers, you may wish to start a prayer journal in which the date you begin to pray for an intention is marked as well as the date this prayer was answered. Consider organizing an intercessory prayer group that meets on a regular basis to pray for specific intentions. This can take the form of a "block rosary" where your neighborhood (or circle of friends and family) meets once per month at someone's house and prays the rosary together for these special intentions—or for the more general intention of world peace.

 Geography

Complete the map started in Chapters 5-7 by labeling the cities red and the countries green. On the map provided, cities are indicated with a star, and countries are in bold capitals.

 Timeline Work

Add the dates and events from 1835 through 1841 to your timeline.

 Checking the Catechism

Read more about prayers of petition and intercessory prayer in the *Catechism of the Catholic Church* text paragraphs 2629-36 and 2647 (195, 315, and 553-554). Read too about prayer groups in text paragraph 2689 (565). Younger students may wish to write their own prayer to Jesus following the instructions for Activity #22 in *100 Activities*. Be sure to include expressions of love, petitions, and words of thanks and praise.

 Searching Scripture

Read what Luke and St. Paul have to say about praying for others and requesting others to pray for you: Acts 12:5, 2 Corinthians 9:13-15, Ephesians 6:18-19, Philippians 1:3-4, Colossians 1:3, Colossians 4:2-3, 2 Thessalonians 1:11-12, and 1 Timothy 2:1-4.

Pauline Jaricot

Chapters 25 through 28—In Which Pauline Funds the Christian Model Town and Then Learns that Her Agent May Not Be Worthy of Trust

 Vocabulary

making *medallions*
She has *implicit* faith
misunderstood and *calumniated*
were *edifying* enough

chapel
Oblate of Mary Immaculate
Sign of the Cross
scandal

Comprehension Questions/Narration Prompts

Chapter 25
1. In the summer of 1845, Marie quoted the membership of the Living Rosary to be about how many people?
2. What did the findings of Pauline's engineer reveal about Rustrel's suitability for the model Christian town?

Chapter 26
1. Despite her reservations, what made Pauline decide to purchase Rustrel? Whom did she appoint as her agent?
2. What did the property at Rustrel cost? What repairs and development needed to be done at additional costs?

Chapter 27
1. What caused Pauline to become concerned about Gustave and the situation at Rustrel? What was John's reaction to Pauline's doubts?
2. On his next trip to Lyons to see Pauline, what was Gustave's new business idea for Rustrel? What was Pauline's reaction to this idea?

Chapter 28
1. How did the Daughters of Mary feel about Gustave?
2. What happened in May of 1846 to finally lead Pauline to agree with her friends' judgment of Gustave's character?

 Forming Opinions/Drawing Conclusions
1. In your opinion (and aided with the vision of hindsight), what could or should Pauline have done differently in her handling of the Rustrel matter?
2. How can Christians, who are required to love others, protect themselves in business affairs without being uncharitable? What virtue must we employ when dealing with our business matters, especially if we are accountable for others' resources?

For Further Study

". . . perhaps we might try our hand at making medallions—the religious type, you know—and distribute them to needy parishes" (page 162). Research the most popular medals that Catholics wear including medals commemorating Sts. Benedict, Christopher and Joseph as well as the Miraculous Medal, Medal of the Holy Face, and the Scapular Medal. Remember that the medal itself has no power; its benefit is the blessing called down from God upon the wearer—beware of superstitious use! Write a brief report on one or more medals of your choice.

 Growing in Holiness

". . . forgive me! I've been most uncharitable!" (page 160) This small exclamation of Pauline's can cause us to examine our own behavior in two areas: first of all, how quick are we to ask for forgiveness when we have wronged someone or injured them in any way? Can we humbly and sincerely ask for forgiveness?

Secondly, we should question ourselves on how charitable our speech is to others. Are we quick to give others the benefit of the doubt—or are we quick to judge them harshly? Do we extend this charitableness only to those we regard as friends or to strangers and enemies alike? Are we equally charitable to those we see each day as opposed to those we do not know as well or see as often?

Be sure to examine your consciences on these points each night, making a good act of contrition for failures, a sincere thanksgiving for God's good grace to persevere, and a firm resolution to amend your sinful habits.

✓ **Checking the Catechism**

Read about the works of the devil, the "father of lies," in the *Catechism of the Catholic Church* in the following text paragraphs: 391, 394-95, 398, and 2846-54 (74-75, 125, and 597). Read also text paragraphs in the *Catechism of the Catholic Church* that teach about prudence: 1788, 1805-06, and 1835 (379-380).

 Searching Scripture

1. Read what Holy Scripture says about prudence: Proverbs 11:14, Proverbs 13:10, and Matthew 10:16. Beware of judging while aided with the vision of hindsight.
2. Read too the story of the deception of the devil in the Garden of Paradise in Genesis 3:1-7.

Chapters 29 through 32—In Which Pauline Begs for Money to Repay the Debts of Rustrel and Suffers Rejection and Humiliation

 Vocabulary

riotous living
to declare you *bankrupt*
arrange for the *mortgages*
house-to-house *canvass*

apparition at La Salette
apparition at *La Salette*
Sacred Heart
Passionist

Comprehension Questions/Narration Prompts

Chapter 29
1. With Gustave back in prison and herself severely in debt, what options did Pauline have? Which of these options did she choose?
2. What did Pauline find upon her arrival at Rustrel? Who did she set in charge of managing Rustrel now?

Chapter 30
1. What caused a setback in the operations at Rustrel? What did Pauline decide to do in response to the creditors' demand for their money?
2. What was Bishop Villecourt's suggestion when Pauline visited him in LaRochelle?

Chapter 31
1. To whom did Pauline confide her true feelings about suffering? What did she say those feelings were?
2. What reaction did Pauline get from the Society for the Propagation of the Faith when she, as their foundress, asked them for assistance?

Chapter 32
1. Despite her rejection by the Society for the Propagation of the Faith, what did Pauline intend to do?
2. What two qualities of Pauline's did Mother Barat most admire?
3. Was Pauline's response from the Lyons committee for the Society for the Propagation of the Faith more encouraging than the response she received from the Paris committee?

 Forming Opinions/Drawing Conclusions
1. Pauline defended the president and council members of the Society for the Propagation of the Faith by asserting that they were not "stupid" but rather "misinformed" (page 187). What is the difference between the two? Would you have been charitable enough to make this distinction?

2. "I do think we have a real saint living with us" (page 191). What qualities, virtues, or attitudes does Mother Barat see in Pauline that prompted her to make this statement? What qualities do you think are important in a saint?
3. Read 1 Corinthians 13:4-7. Give examples from Pauline's actions and attitude that address each clause of verses 5 and 6 of the above citation.
4. Do you agree with Maria that the poor have a different attitude toward charity and sacrifice (page 191)? Support your answer.

 For Further Study

Research two contemporaries of Pauline Jaricot: Madeleine Sophie Barat, the foundress of the Religious of the Sacred Heart, and John Henry Newman, the famous Anglican convert. Write short biography of one or both of these saints.

 Growing in Holiness

1. In Our Lady's apparition at La Salette, France, in 1846, the Blessed Virgin spoke of her sadness that so many people were working on Sundays and neglecting the sacraments. Review how your family spends Sunday. Is it just another day in the weekend? Is it a day set aside for God? Is needless work and shopping avoided on this day? Is it truly a day dedicated to God and spent in rest and praise for His many blessings? Research this commandment of God and discuss with your parents what your family might do to improve your use of this day.
2. Read how the apostles, after their scourging, went "rejoicing" that they had been found worthy to suffer for the sake of Jesus' name in Acts 5:40-41. How can we strengthen ourselves so that we, like the apostles and like Pauline Jaricot, will be willing to suffer dishonor and humiliation for Jesus?

 Timeline Work

Add the dates and events from 1845 through 1850 to your timeline.

✓ **Checking the Catechism**

Discover what the *Catechism of the Catholic Church* has to say about the third commandment in text paragraphs 2168-95 (289 and 450-454). You may also wish to read Pope John Paul II's encyclical issued in 1998, *Dies Domini (On Keeping the Lord's Day Holy)*, found at www.ewtn.com/library/PAPALDOC/JP2DIES.HTM.

 **Searching Scripture**

Read the following biblical texts related to the keeping of the Sabbath—or as expressed in Revelation (Apocalypse) 1:10, the "Lord's day": Exodus 20:8-11, Exodus 31:12-17, Matthew 12:1-8, and Mark 3:4.

Chapters 33 through 36—In Which Pauline Continues to Struggle with Debt, Humiliation, and Slander

 Vocabulary

a religious *fanatic*
a great *boon*
not to be *dissuaded*
physical *infirmities*

Portress
Lourdes
Vicar
Eternal City

Comprehension Questions/Narration Prompts

Chapter 33
1. What disappointment awaited Pauline when she returned to Loreto in the fall of 1850? What decision was she forced to make to help cover her debts? How well did this plan work?
2. What new idea was suggested to Pauline to help obtain money to apply to her debts?

Chapter 34
1. What did Pauline ruefully call her "certificate of nobility"?
2. What did Pauline believe was part of the Divine Plan for her life?
3. Why did Pauline decide to travel to Rome in the summer of 1856?

Chapter 35
1. How were Pauline and Maria received at the home of Pauline's long-time friend in Marseilles?
2. How did Pauline react to this reception?

Chapter 36
1. How was Pauline received by Pope Pius IX?
2. What was the unpleasant situation that awaited Pauline upon her return from Rome in December of 1856?

 Forming Opinions/Drawing Conclusions

1. Why do you think the Society for the Propagation of the Faith would advise people not to contribute any money to Pauline? Be charitable!
2. What virtues or holy habits would it take to react as Pauline Jaricot did to the rejection of her friend? How can these virtues and habits be developed?
3. How do you think Pauline will try to resolve the situation with her unpleasant neighbor Mademoiselle Roccofort?

✝ Growing in Holiness

As a way of learning about the virtues of Venerable Pauline Jaricot—in order to better imitate them—privately recite her litany as proscribed below. (obtained from www.catholicdoors.com)

Lord, have mercy on us. *Christ, have mercy on us.* Lord, have mercy on us. *Christ, graciously hear us.* God the Father of Heaven, *have mercy on us.* God the Holy Spirit, *have mercy on us.* Holy Trinity, One God, *have mercy on us.* Holy Mary, *pray for us.* [Repeat *pray for us* at each asterisk.] Venerable Pauline Marie Jaricot, Faithful imitator of Jesus Christ, *. Faithful to domestic and family duties, *. Faithful adorer of the Most Blessed Sacrament, *. Persecuted to the fullness of martyrdom, *. Entirely detached from perishable possessions, *. Virgin Spouse of Jesus Christ, Ardent in the praise of the Infinite Love of the Divine Eucharist, *. Dedicated to the extension of the Kingdom of Jesus Christ throughout the whole world, *. Undaunted by the cost of personal sacrifice for the salvation of souls, *. Guided by the motto "God alone and His greater glory," *. Pauline, whose work was blessed with miraculous success, *. Whose life gave joy to the Hearts of Jesus and Mary, *. Whose life was one of continual prayer, *. Who was the match, which lit the fire of faith universally, *. Who knew no compromise, *. For whom no task was too great, *. Who suffered the fury of Hell, *. Who suffered the martyrdom of contradictions, calumnies and scorn, *. Who was abandoned by all, *. Whom God has loaded with crosses and great graces, *. Whose charity was inexhaustible, *. Who was miraculously cured through the intercession of St. Philomena, *. Who suffered the loss of every human consolation, *. Who was obedient and mortified, *. Whose trust in God never faltered, *. Who pardoned, loved and prayed for those who caused her ruin, *. Who united the contemplative life to an active life of good works, *. Whose sanctity was anchored in absolute submission to the will and pleasure of thy Divine Master, *. Whose only baggage and treasure upon this earth was the Cross, *. Who suffered ill health with perfect resignation, *. Whose last agony was long and cruel, *. Who hast given thy heart to the Heart of Jesus, *. Who breathed forth thy soul to the Mother of God, *. Heart of Pauline, Furnace of charity, *. Enlightened guide of souls, *. Comforter of the afflicted, *. Admirable adorer of Jesus in the Most Blessed Sacrament, *. Constant in prayer for the sanctification of the priesthood, *. Purified and tried as purest gold in the crucible of suffering, *. Burning ceaselessly for the salvation of souls, *. Mother of the Propagation of the Faith, *. Mother of thy Living Rosary, *. Mother of souls, *. Mother of happy deaths, *. Mother of those who suffer poverty, *. Pauline Marie, Heroic in thy virtues, *. Heroic in thy suffering, *. Heroic in thy love, *. Faithful and obedient daughter of the Holy Roman Catholic Church, *. Lamb of God, who takes away the sins of the world, *Spare us, O Lord.* Lamb of God, who takes away the sins of the world, *Graciously hear us O Lord.* Lamb of God, who takes away the sins of the world, *Have mercy on us, O Lord.* Heart of Jesus, *hear us.* Heart of Jesus, *graciously hear us.* Pray for us, O venerable Pauline Marie Jaricot, *that we may be worthy of the promises of Christ.* Let us pray. Almighty and merciful God, Who has chosen a humble virgin, Pauline Marie of Jesus Christ, the poor one of Mary, to found the great Catholic works of the Propagation of the Faith and the Living Rosary, and Who has wished in the midst of humiliations, trials and persecutions to purify her works, deign to hasten the day when the Church will recognize publicly her saintly life. We pray, that by her example of patience and love of the Cross, her lifetime prayer will be realized in its fullness: Propagation of the Faith in all its purity throughout the world! Amen.

Chapters 37 through 41—In Which Pauline Fully Accepts Her Suffering, Prepares to Die, and Breathes Her Last

 Vocabulary

threw *discretion* to the winds
as though in a *trance*
a severe case of *dropsy*
keeping constant *vigil*

Way of the Cross
Last Day
ecstasy
Cenacle

??? Comprehension Questions/Narration Prompts

Chapter 37
1. How was the situation of the two paths to the shrine resolved by the court? Was it really resolved?
2. What was the Society for the Propagation of the Faith's response to the Holy Father's request that they help Pauline financially?
3. Why did Pauline decide to go to Ars in March of 1859? Why did the carriage driver refuse to take her and Maria all the way there?

Chapter 38
1. What was the "baggage" that Pauline brought with her to Ars?
2. According to Father Vianney, what is "one of the greatest gifts in heaven's treasury"?
3. What did Father John Vianney claim is our greatest suffering in this life?

Chapter 39
1. In relation to Pauline's visit to Ars, when did Father John Vianney die? How long had he been a priest?
2. As Pauline neared death, what did she consider an issue of importance to think about and sacrifice for?

Chapter 40
1. What book was Pauline studying during her last days? What was the premise of this book?
2. What does Pauline call "a little foretaste of heaven"?

Chapter 41
What were Pauline Jaricot's last words?

 Forming Opinions/Drawing Conclusions
1. "Pennies for Pauline," as quoted on page 220, was the title of the original edition of this book by Mary Fabyan Windeatt when it was first published in 1952. Why was

this title appropriate? What did it signify about Pauline's life and the societies she founded?
2. What do you think it means to be "warmed in spirit" as mentioned by Pauline on page 227?
3. "God is my witness, Jesus Christ is my model, Mary is my support. I ask nothing but love and sacrifice" (page 229). How can you live this motto every day?
4. Why do you think Maria Candas said of Pauline, "Some day people will be calling her the patron saint of failures" (page 238)? Is this an appropriate title for Pauline Jaricot? Explain your answer.
5. Explain the image of the two lamps as presented on page 240.
6. Why did Maria not want to tell Pauline that her nephew had a plan to pay off the debt?

Growing in Holiness

On page 233, Pauline speaks of the three tools of a stay-at-home missionary: the Holy Sacrifice of the Mass, prayer—especially the rosary—and almsgiving. To begin a serious apostolate of missionary activity from your home, begin to use all three of these tools on a regular basis. Try to attend daily Mass, pray the rosary every day, and financially support missionary efforts. Remember that St. Thérèse of Lisieux was declared the patroness of foreign missions—and she was a cloistered nun! You may want to make your intentions general, or research and choose a particular country for which to pray. Save souls!

Geography

If desired, use a modern map to locate the countries not labeled on your map. Mark each country as its boundaries exist today.

Timeline Work

Add the dates and events from 1852 through 1919 to complete your timeline.

✓ Checking the Catechism

Read about the lay faithful—their vocation and participation in the mission of the Church and in evangelization—in the *Catechism of the Catholic Church*, text paragraphs 897-901 and 904-905 (80, 172-173, 184, and 190).

Searching Scripture

"[Our Lady] had nothing in her old age either, you know, and had to be looked after by others" (page 236). Read John 19:25-27.

Book Summary Test for *Pauline Jaricot*

Directions: Answer in complete sentences. If necessary, use the back of the page for additional writing space. 100 possible points, 20 points for each answer.

1. Name the two organizations that Pauline Jaricot founded that still exist today. In what other charitable works was she involved?

2. Pauline was cured of a serious heart condition by the intercession of which saint? Name three notable Catholic figures who were contemporaries of Pauline.

3. What project of Pauline's caused not only humiliation but incurred a large debt? How did this debt come about?

4. What were some of the strong character traits of Pauline Jaricot? In what vocation was Pauline—married, single, or religious?

5. Pauline suffered many setbacks and humiliations. Using examples from the book, describe how her life and attitude reflected that of John the Baptist when he said about Jesus, "He must increase; I must decrease" (John 3:30). How can you imitate Pauline Jaricot in your own daily life?

Pauline Jaricot, Foundress of the Living Rosary and the Society for the Propagation of the Faith

Answer Key to Comprehension Questions

Chapters 1 through 4—In Which Young Pauline Suffers, Recovers from Her Accident, and Tries to Find God's Plan for Her Life

Chapter 1
1. Pauline Jaricot was born in 1799 and lived in France.
2. When Pauline was fourteen and fifteen years old, she thought mostly of her social life, marriage, clothes, and how she looked.

Chapter 2
1. Due to her poor health, Pauline was not told about her mother's death or her brother Paul's marriage.
2. Pauline went from a normal, healthy fifteen-year-old girl to a girl so sick that the doctor did not feel she would ever fully recover.

Chapter 3
1. Pauline showed a marked improvement after talking to a priest and receiving the sacraments of Confession and Holy Communion.
2. Pauline could not imagine herself as a nun in a convent as she liked traveling and nice clothes too much.
3. Pauline was hoping that this priest would "straighten me out" (page 18).

Chapter 4
1. While Pauline's family was pleased with her happiness and contentment, they felt she spent too much time in prayer and works of charity. They felt she was "going to extremes" (page 20).
2. Pauline was hoping that her sacrifices might purify her to hear the voice of God so she would finally know what the work was that He had prepared for her for all eternity. Her new sacrifice was to wear purple—the color she hated the most—every day.

Chapters 5 through 7—In Which Pauline Begins Her Mission despite All Obstacles

Chapter 5
1. Pauline decided to provide any help she could to the female workers at her brother-in-law's silk factory. Her spiritual director Father Wurtz supported her in this, the girls responded well to her, and her brother Phileas began to have a "conversion" of his own.
2. Both of his children seemed to be developing vocations to the religious life, and he was confused and afraid.
3. He decided to go see Father Charles Balley and his assistant Father John Vianney to seek advice and prayers.

Chapter 6
1. Pauline's accomplishments at the factory include the following:
    a. She had made personal friends with the girls.
    b. She had brought many of them back to the Church.
    c. The factory workers stopped to pray each day at three o'clock.
    d. She had elevated the spirit of the workers.
    e. She had formed a society—the Reparatrices of the Heart of Jesus.
2. For the missions in China, Pauline organized the effort to raise from each worker one penny a week.
3. Phileas' announcement of his intention to study for the priesthood gave the society a sign that their prayers and sacrifices were being answered and rewarded. They were pleased, proud, and renewed.

4. Father Wurtz advised Pauline to spend some time each day in prayer before the Blessed Sacrament. (Mother Teresa, as busy as she was, always spent several hours each day before the Blessed Sacrament—more on those days she was especially busy.)

Chapter 7
1. Pauline's father could not understand how she could be happy with her new friends, her new wardrobe, and the endless work. He worried about her future.
2. Pauline's new inspiration was to divide the contributors into groups of ten, groups of a hundred, groups of a thousand—each with their own leader. Before implementing this idea, she sought the approval and permission of her pastor.

Chapters 8 through 10—In Which Pauline Is Beset By Obstacles and Begins the Association of the Living Rosary

Chapter 8
1. Monsignor Gourdiat believed that the devil would cause trouble as the work was beginning to prosper and grow. He stated, "Suffering always accompanies any worthwhile work" (page 47).
2. As Pauline continued to work for the missions, people began to say that she was doing the priest's work or only working for the publicity. Some people believed that she was insane to dress so plainly and not be interested in marriage.
3. Pauline began each day with Mass at four o'clock followed by bookkeeping for the Propagation of the Faith, caring for the sick in the hospital, visiting the poor and imprisoned, and keeping company with her father. She often prayed long into the night.
4. Victor and Pauline felt that they had promised themselves and their friends to the work in China. Furthermore, they were suspicious of Father Inglesi, the priest from America.

Chapter 9
1. The compromise reached between Pauline and several members of the Propagation for the Society of the Faith that allowed funds to also be given to the American missions was for a worldwide society to be formed under the guidance of a new committee. On May 3, 1822, the society that Pauline had founded was reorganized to include the missions of the whole world. Pauline no longer had a leading role in the society.
2. The Society for the Propagation of the Faith grew enough to warrant two central offices: one in Lyons and the other in Paris. Pope Pius VII gave his blessing to the society that required each member to daily recite one Our Father and one Hail Mary plus the ejaculation, "St. Francis Xavier, pray for us." One penny per week was also required of each member.
3. Pauline was suspicious of Father Inglesi while many others trusted him. He was proven, however, to be an impostor and made off with a considerable amount of the society's money.

Chapter 10
1. Pauline's spiritual director Father Wurtz advised her, primarily for health reasons, to give up all outside activities for three years.
2. Pauline offered herself as a victim for sinners. Father Wurtz did not approve as he felt God wanted her to live.
3. The idea of a Living Rosary—an association of prayer—was conceived as a way to pray for the future of France and its children.

Chapters 11 through 15—In Which Both Pauline's Sister and Brother Die, and She Herself Becomes Seriously Ill

Chapter 11
1. The objectives of the Living Rosary were to bring the people of France back to a prayerful way of life through the recitation of the rosary, and to promote good reading habits (as urged by Pope Leo XII).
2. Objections to the recitation of the rosary that Pauline encountered included the following: seeing no point in reciting the Hail Mary over and over, its childishness, the tendency of the mind to wander during this prayer, the objection of reciting rote prayers rather than speak-

ing directly to God in one's own words, and the view that the recitation of the rosary is a "chore."
3. Pauline countered these objections by pointing out that there is more merit in offering a prayer that is difficult for us rather than one of our own choosing. In addition, it is the prayer preferred by the Blessed Virgin so out of love we should be willing to provide it for her. Pauline also stated that we imitate the pleasing words of the archangel Gabriel when we pray the Hail Mary.

Chapter 12
1. Pauline's brother Father Phileas was poisoned twice at the hospital where he served as head chaplain. He was poisoned as the staff felt he was initiating too many changes. Some of his new rules were not liked; he had dismissed several long-time employees. "He was too much the reformer" (page 75).
2. Although he wished to be a foreign missionary, Pauline's brother Phileas was a chaplain in a Lyons' hospital due to his poor health. Twice the staff of the hospital poisoned him; the second time, in the spring of 1830, it was fatal.

Chapter 13
1. Pauline purchased a large house outside of Lyons, which she named "Loreto" after the house of the Holy Family. She used this house as the headquarters of the Association of the Living Rosary. It was large enough to be used as storage space for the association's records and collection of pamphlets, books, and religious articles for the needy. The nurses entrusted to Pauline's care after the death of Phileas came to live at Loreto, allowing the house of Nazareth to be converted into a hospital for incurables, or what we would now call "hospice care."
2. To show his appreciation for the generous financial support that the Jaricots had given him, Father de Magallon of the Brothers of St. John of God brought Pauline a relic of Philomena. This relic, the only one like it in France, was housed in Loreto. Pauline and her friends began immediately to pray for the canonization of Philomena who was responsible for so many cures and conversions in Ars, the parish of John Vianney.

Chapter 14
1. Pauline and her friends (those living at Loreto) were forced to evacuate Loreto in 1834 due to the uprising of the working class at that time. The working class rose against the factory owners, and government troops were called in to quell the disturbance. For several days, the city was taken over by rioters; bullets and cannon shells could be seen and heard. The residents of Loreto spent three days in a cave on Pauline's property.
2. The occupants of the cave felt protected and safe as they had taken the tabernacle from the chapel with them to the cave.

Chapter 15
1. Over five hundred people were killed in the workers' uprising in Lyons in 1834. Government troops put down the workers who returned to work with no change of working conditions.
2. Pauline wished to travel to Mugnano near Naples, a journey of six hundred miles by stagecoach, in order to make a pilgrimage to the tomb of Philomena. She felt that Philomena would cure her there. Pauline also wanted to stop in Rome to talk to the Holy Father regarding the Association of the Living Rosary.

Chapters 16 through 20—In Which Pauline Is Cured of Her Heart Condition by the Intercession of St. Philomena

Chapter 16
1. In addition to founding both the Society for the Propagation of the Faith and the Association of the Living Rosary, Pauline also was generous in her financial support of several religious communities, worked closely with the problems of the working class, and housed over twenty needy girls and women at Loreto.
2. In Rome in the summer of 1835, Pope Gregory XVI made an agreement with Pauline at Madeleine Sophie Barat's convent. He agreed to do something for Philomena's cause for canonization if Pauline were to be cured at Philomena's shrine in Mugnano.

3. When Pauline arrived at Philomena's shrine in Mugnano, Italy, in August of 1835, the townspeople demanded a miracle of Philomena. They demanded that she cure Pauline.

Chapter 17
1. Pauline expressed only relief and a childlike joy when she felt she was about to die in August of 1835.
2. Through the intercession of Philomena, Pauline was cured of her heart and breathing problems.

Chapter 18
1. In Mugnano, Pauline participated in many public celebrations of her cure by Philomena. Pauline "conquered her fatigue, overcame her shyness, obeyed orders, and was rewarded by a peace and joy such as she had never before experienced" (page 107).
2. In Naples the Papal Nuncio predicted that Pauline would do great things for souls—that God would make use of her for this purpose. He also predicted that she would need to bear many crosses in her work for God.
3. Pope Gregory XVI gave permission for Pauline to build a chapel in Lyons in honor of Philomena. Now that Pauline had been cured, he also promised an immediate study of Philomena's cause for canonization.

Chapter 19
1. In Rome, Pauline secured the permission of the Master General of the Dominican Order to affiliate the Association of the Living Rosary with the Dominican order.
2. Marie was uneasy about the Living Rosary adopting St. Dominic as a patron because St. Dominic had to suffer so much in his own work. She felt that the members of the Living Rosary might have to suffer as St. Dominic did in order for their work to succeed.

Chapter 20
1. While in Italy, Pauline had sent a relic of Philomena to Father John Vianney.
2. Father Vianney insisted that the cures and conversions taking place in Ars were not due to his own intercession but to the intercession of St. John the Baptist and St. John Francis Regis (his patron saints), St. Michael the Archangel, and St. Philomena.
3. St. Philomena was canonized in January of 1837. Her feast day was set for August 11th.

Chapters 21 through 24—In Which Pauline Outlines the Plan for the Holy Childhood Association and Moves Forward in Her Plans to Develop a Model Christian Town

Chapter 21
1. Marie Melquiond felt that many people were jealous of Pauline because she was an intelligent woman who had been very successful in her ventures. She felt there was resentment that someone who was not a priest or man, but indeed a single woman, had founded two very important works for the Church.
2. Pauline's new idea, which had the bishop's full support, was that Catholic children should make weekly contributions in much the same way as the adults did for the Propagation of the Faith. This money would then be used to rescue unwanted Chinese babies from an unbaptized death. This new organization was to be called the Association of the Holy Childhood.

Chapter 22
1. The Bank of Heaven, as instituted by Pauline Jaricot, was an association of fifteen of Pauline's wealthy friends who would lend twenty thousand dollars each to form an initial capital fund for her Christian model town.
2. Pauline bore the heavy cross of not receiving any support for her almsgiving or charitable projects from her family. Her main supporters, her brother Phileas and her two sisters Laurette and Sophie as well as her father, were now dead. Her brother Paul and brother-in-law Victor were generally not in favor of her charities.
3. Paul did not trust John Allioud as John had recently declared bankruptcy. Although John's wife and daughter were working to pay off the debts, John himself was not employed. Paul called him "an impractical fool" (page 132).

Chapter 23
1. In an effort to cheer her melancholy friend John Allioud, Pauline suggested that he invite his friend Gustave Perre to come visit John and his family at Nazareth.
2. When Pauline discovered that Gustave Perre was in prison for financial troubles, she volunteered to give John the money necessary to help pay Gustave's debts.

Chapter 24
The women of Loreto were less enthusiastic about Gustave Perre when they found out he had recently been in prison. His polished speech, extreme politeness, and over-eagerness to please Pauline also worried Pauline's friend Constance.

Chapters 25 through 28—In Which Pauline Funds the Christian Model Town and then Learns that Her Agent May Not Be Worthy of Her Trust

Chapter 25
1. In the summer of 1845, Marie quoted the membership of the Association of the Living Rosary at approximately three million members.
2. Pauline's engineer, who inspected the property at Rustrel, noted rich quantities of iron ore, valuable deposits of clay, a fine tract of timber, a flour mill, workingman's quarters, four iron ore blast furnaces, and a little chapel dedicated to Our Lady of the Angels—just as Gustave Perre had claimed.

Chapter 26
1. Despite her reservations, Pauline agreed to purchase Rustrel when Gustave stated that the sale of Rustrel would be forced within a day or two. Gustave insisted that it would be in her best interests to work through an agent, so Pauline made Gustave her agent.
2. The purchase price of Rustrel was ninety thousand dollars; in addition, several repairs were required including repairs to the blast furnace and the mill. Several acres needed to be cultivated and sown, and the chapel needed cleaning and redecorating.

Chapter 27
1. Pauline became concerned about Gustave's integrity and the situation at Rustrel when she began receiving disturbing, anonymous letters from some people around Rustrel warning Pauline not to trust Gustave. These people claimed that Gustave was spending her money improperly and not managing Rustrel well. Pauline discussed this with John who was very hurt that she would believe such things about his friend Gustave. John offered to go to Rustrel himself to investigate; he soon wrote Pauline that all was well at Rustrel.
2. On his next trip to see Pauline, Gustave suggested that they begin making religious medallions at Rustrel. This new business idea would require new equipment. Pauline generously agreed to pay whatever extra expenses this exciting new venture would require.

Chapter 28
1. Members of Pauline's informal religious community, the Daughters of Mary, had felt an aversion to Gustave from the beginning. They did not trust him and did not feel that he was qualified or capable of managing Pauline's affairs in Rustrel.
2. In May of 1846 Pauline received a letter from Gustave defending himself against his association with people of questionable reputations. However, the general tone of his letter was very defensive and defiant. It prompted Pauline to admit that she had made a mistake in ever placing her trust in Gustave Perre. She decided to send no further money to him and, against doctor's orders, would go to see Rustrel for herself.

Chapters 29 through 32—In Which Pauline Begs for Money to Repay the Debts of Rustrel and Suffers Rejection and Humiliation

Chapter 29
1. With Gustave back in prison and herself severely in debt, Pauline had several options: bankruptcy, which would free her of any claim her debtors had on her; the sale of Rustrel; or a mortgage on both Rustrel and Loreto. She chose to keep her promises—even those made through her agent—and obtain mortgages on both Rustrel and Loreto.

2. Upon her arrival at Rustrel, Pauline found that Gustave had done almost nothing to put the place in order. The chapel especially was in poor shape. Maria's brother Peter Dubouis was placed as manager in charge of Rustrel.

Chapter 30
1. The workers' revolution of 1848 caused a setback in the operations at Rustrel. Factory workers again stormed the streets, dissatisfied with poor wages and miserable living conditions. As France seemed to be approaching financial and political ruin, the creditors of the mortgages on Rustrel and Loreto demanded principal payments in addition to the interest payments that were being made, or foreclosure would be unavoidable. In response, Pauline decided to go about the country begging for money to pay the debts.
2. Bishop Villecourt, a long-time friend of Pauline's, suggested that she consider any money she raised as a donation rather than a loan to be paid back. He further suggested that she contact the Society for the Propagation of the Faith, with whom Pauline had not had any contact for over twenty-six years. The bishop felt that the members might be willing to help Pauline pay off her debts and in fact wrote a letter of recommendation to the society on Pauline's behalf.

Chapter 31
1. Pauline confided to Madeleine Sophie Barat, with whom she stayed while in Paris, that she *loathed* suffering. Pauline stated that she had never been able to conquer her desire for fine things.
2. When Pauline, as foundress of the Society for the Propagation of the Faith, asked to discuss the Rustrel project with the society in hopes of obtaining financial backing, she was told that she was not the foundress of the society. A poor servant girl from Lyons whose name has since been forgotten was the recognized foundress. The current president of the society would not let Pauline discuss the Rustrel project with the other members until he was able to discuss the matter with the council.

Chapter 32
1. Despite her rejection by the Society for the Propagation of the Faith, Pauline intended to continue to attempt to raise the necessary money to pay off her debts. She planned to stay in Paris for a year, conducting a door-to-door canvass for money.
2. Mother Barat stated that she has never met an equal to Pauline Jaricot. She especially admired Pauline's charity and resignation.
3. The committee from Lyons agreed with the Paris committee of the Society for the Propagation of the Faith in rejecting Pauline's claim as foundress. The Lyons committee accused Pauline of being a "misguided woman" (page 193) and refused to give any assistance to Pauline.

Chapters 33 through 36—In Which Pauline Continues to Struggle with Debt, Humiliation and Slander

Chapter 33
1. When Pauline returned from Paris in the fall of 1850, she found that many members of the Daughters of Mary at Loreto had left to join other religious communities. Discouraged by this and by the lack of progress in her fund-raising efforts, she decided she must sell Rustrel. However when sold, Rustrel only yielded one-third of the original purchase price.
2. A roadway contractor suggested to Pauline that she build a path so that pilgrims could take a short cut through her property to Our Lady's shrine in Fourvière. Hundreds of pilgrims traveled to the shrine each day. If each pilgrim paid one penny for the short cut, money could be raised toward the debt.

Chapter 34
1. When Pauline received written notification that she and her community were eligible for public charity from the parish, she lightheartedly called it her "certificate of nobility."
2. Pauline believed that her poverty, her persecution, and the lies that were being told about her as well as her health problems were all part of the Divine Plan. She believed that they were the price God was asking of her in return for the success of the Society for the Propagation of the Faith and the Living Rosary Association.

3. In the summer of 1856, Pauline decided to travel to Rome to see Pope Pius IX. She felt she needed to explain to him the circumstances surrounding the dispute regarding her founding of the Society for the Propagation of the Faith as now not only her reputation but that of Count de Brémond and his wife were at risk.

Chapter 35
1. Pauline's friend in Marseilles not only refused to accommodate her in her home but refused to even speak to her.
2. Pauline accepted this rebuff with her usual calm composure, refusing to judge her friend or her friend's actions.

Chapter 36
1. Pope Pius IX received Pauline cordially and with complete understanding of her situation. He indicated that he would contact the Paris office of the Society for the Propagation of the Faith encouraging them to help Pauline pay off her debts. He also offered to take care of all her expenses for her return trip to Loreto in Lyons.
2. Upon Pauline's return to Lyons from Rome, she discovered that her neighbor had taken advantage of Pauline's absence and had built a shorter path to the shrine. However, this path was partially on Pauline's property. When Pauline approached her to resolve the situation, the neighbor became unreasonable, resorting to name-calling and threatening to fight Pauline "every inch of the way" (page 216).

Chapters 37 through 41—In Which Pauline Fully Accepts Her Suffering, Prepares to Die, and Breathes Her Last

Chapter 37
1. When the issue of the two paths was taken to court, the court ruled in favor of Pauline, asking Mademoiselle Roccofort to close her path at once and stop seeking money from the pilgrims. Unfortunately, Mademoiselle Roccofort disregarded the court order, kept her path open, and continued to collect the toll from the pilgrims.
2. In response to the Holy Father's request that they assist Pauline financially, the Society for the Propagation of the Faith took the attitude that they were not bound to obey the Holy Father as this was not a matter involving faith and morals.
3. Pauline decided to go to Ars in March of 1859 as her creditors, the pilgrims, and the Fourvière Commission were all heavily pressuring her. She wanted to spend time talking with her friend John Vianney, the parish priest of Ars. The carriage driver refused to continue the journey to Ars as a snowstorm began, and he was concerned that he would not manage the snowdrifts.

Chapter 38
1. The "baggage" Pauline brought to Ars was her troubles—her concern for the debt, her rejection by others, her humiliations.
2. According to Father Vianney, one of the greatest gifts in heaven's treasury is "an *understanding* of the Way of the Cross, a *love* of trials and suffering" (page 227).
3. According to Father John Vianney, our greatest suffering in this life is our fear of suffering.

Chapter 39
1. Less than five months after Pauline's visit to Ars in March of 1859—on August 4th—Father John Vianney died. He had been a priest for forty-four years, most of them as the Curé of Ars.
2. An important issue for Pauline as she neared death was to think about and sacrifice for souls—"the pagan souls of this nineteenth century and the centuries yet to come" (page 232).

Chapter 40
1. During her last days, Pauline read and studied Louis de Montfort's *True Devotion to the Blessed Virgin Mary*—a book that is still in print today (under the title of *True Devotion to Mary*). This book contains de Montfort's doctrine "that a very sure and simple way to gain heaven is to give oneself and all one's possessions into Our Lady's hands for her to do with as she pleases; to become her slave, so to speak, and through her, the slave of Jesus" (page 237).

2. Pauline calls friendship, the really honest kind, "a little foretaste of heaven" (page 238).
Chapter 41
Pauline Jaricot's last words before she died were "Mary, my Mother, I am all yours" (page 242).

Answer Key to Book Summary Test

1. The two organizations that Pauline Jaricot founded that still exist today are the Society for the Propagation of the Faith and the Living Rosary Association. She also suggested the idea of the Holy Childhood Association. Several of her good works include generous alms to various religious communities, interest and activity with the working class, and the house of Loreto which housed twenty or more women and girls who received free room and board.
2. Pauline was cured of a serious heart condition by the intercession of St. Philomena; this cure was instrumental in bringing about the canonization of St. Philomena. Other notable Catholic figures mentioned in this book who were contemporaries of Pauline include St. John Vianney, St. Madeleine Sophie Barat, St. John Newman, Pope Gregory XVI, Pope Pius VII, and Pope Pius IX. (Pope Pius VIII was pope for only one year.)
3. Pauline's idea of a model Christian town at Rustrel caused much heartache and humiliation in her life. It was not that the idea was not a good idea; however, she employed an untrustworthy agent who misused her funds and incurred a debt that amounted to more than Pauline's financial assets.
4. Pauline Jaricot had many fine character traits including the following: humility, honesty, generosity, patience, and finally a love of suffering. She strongly exhibited all three of the theological virtues of faith, hope, and love. Pauline accomplished her works of charity and mission work as a single woman; she never married nor did she feel called to the religious state.
5. Answers will vary.

Note: The year following Pauline's death, the Fourvière Commission purchased the property at Loreto. This money, supplemented by funds from Pauline's nephews (including Ernest), was sufficient to pay Pauline's debt in full.

Study Guide for

*Saint Paul the Apostle,
The Story of the
Apostle to the Gentiles*

St. Paul

Saul was born in Tarsus, Cilicia—the son of a Jew.
The laws of the prophets and Torah he knew.
Tent-maker by trade,
A man on crusade,
The followers of Christ into prison he threw.

On the road to Damascus, this Christ he did meet.
An encounter so strong knocked him off his feet.
Blind, weak, he was led,
Spent three days in bed,
Cured by a Christian, to the desert did retreat.

Saul prayed and did penance—a hermit's life he led,
Then went to Damascus the Good News to spread.
 So outspoken was he
At night had to flee.
As a speaker for Christ, first of many times he fled.

A preacher and teacher, Saul traveled a lot.
His fellow Jews did not accept what he taught.
To the Gentiles he turned.
Many miles he sojourned.
Became known as *Paul* as their acceptance he sought.

On three separate journeys, Paul traveled about,
Taught about the Messiah the Empire throughout.
Much time did devote
To letters he wrote.
Paul made many friends—and many foes—en route.

The Jews tried to kill him, spoke heresy said they.
Paul's Roman citizenship kept them at bay.
Till Nero went mad,
Saw Christians as bad,
Killed Paul and St. Peter upon the same day.

Think what you can learn from this saint and his tale.
How you can apply it to help you prevail.
Then mold what you do
And boldly pursue
His pattern of holiness. Follow his trail.

Timeline of Events

Year	Event
44 BC	Death of Julius Caesar by group of Romans led by Brutus and Cassius
27 BC	Caesar Augustus (Octavian) becomes the first Roman Emperor, beginning the *Pax Romana* or Roman peace, that was to aid the spread of Christianity
4 BC	Approximate date of the birth of Jesus Christ
7 BC	Approximate date of the birth of Saul of Tarsus, a Roman citizen and a Jew
14 AD	Tiberius I becomes Emperor of Rome (until 37)
22	Saul moves to Jerusalem to study under Gamaliel, a teacher of the law
30	Approximate date of the crucifixion of Jesus Christ
34	Stephen, a deacon, stoned to death in Jerusalem; beginning of persecution of Church in Jerusalem which aided the spread of Christianity as many Christians fled Jerusalem, relocating in Judea, Samaria, Syria, and Cyprus; conversion of Saul of Tarsus on the road to Damascus; retires to Arabia
37	Saul returns to Damascus to preach, stays briefly in Jerusalem, then retreats to Tarsus; persecution of the Church slackens allowing the Faith to flourish, Caligula (Gaius Caesar) becomes Emperor of Rome (until 41)
41	Herod Agrippa becomes King of Judea; Claudius I, Emperor of Rome (to 54)
42	Barnabas seeks out Saul, who then accompanies him to Antioch to preach
44	Persecution of Church again breaks out under Herod; James, son of Zebedee, martyred; famine in Jerusalem; Herod's death leads to period of peace
45	Saul and Barnabas, accompanied by Barnabas' nephew Mark, begin their first missionary journey to Cyprus and Asia Minor
48	Paul and Barnabas return to Antioch after traveling over one thousand miles
49	Council of Jerusalem
51	Paul writes the first book of the New Testament—a letter to the Thessalonians
50-52	Paul's second missionary journey to Asia Minor, Macedonia, and Greece
53	Paul begins his third missionary journey accompanied by Timothy and Titus
54	Nero becomes Emperor of Rome; Antonius Felix becomes procurator of Judea
57	After two years in Ephesus, Paul goes to Philippi, then travels to Corinth
58	In the spring, Paul makes plans to go to Jerusalem where he is arrested; suffers imprisonment for two years in Caesarea under Felix
60	Paul travels as a prisoner by ship to Rome; shipwrecked, he arrives in Rome in the spring of 61; stays until his release in June of 63, then travels to Crete
64	Fire destroys much of Rome; Nero blames the Christians; first general persecution of Christians begins (to 68); Paul journeys to Ephesus and Spain (?)
65	Paul returns to Rome briefly; travels around Asia Minor, Macedonia, and Greece, returning to Rome around 67
67	Beheading of St. Paul in Rome; Peter crucified in Rome at this same time
68	After suicide of Nero, Galba becomes Roman emperor (to 69)
69	Year of four emperors in Rome, the last being Vespasian (to 79)
70	Destruction of Jerusalem, aids in Christianity's separation from Judaism
95	Second general persecution of Christians begins (until 96) under Emperor Domitian (81-96); John the Evangelist and Pope Clement I martyred

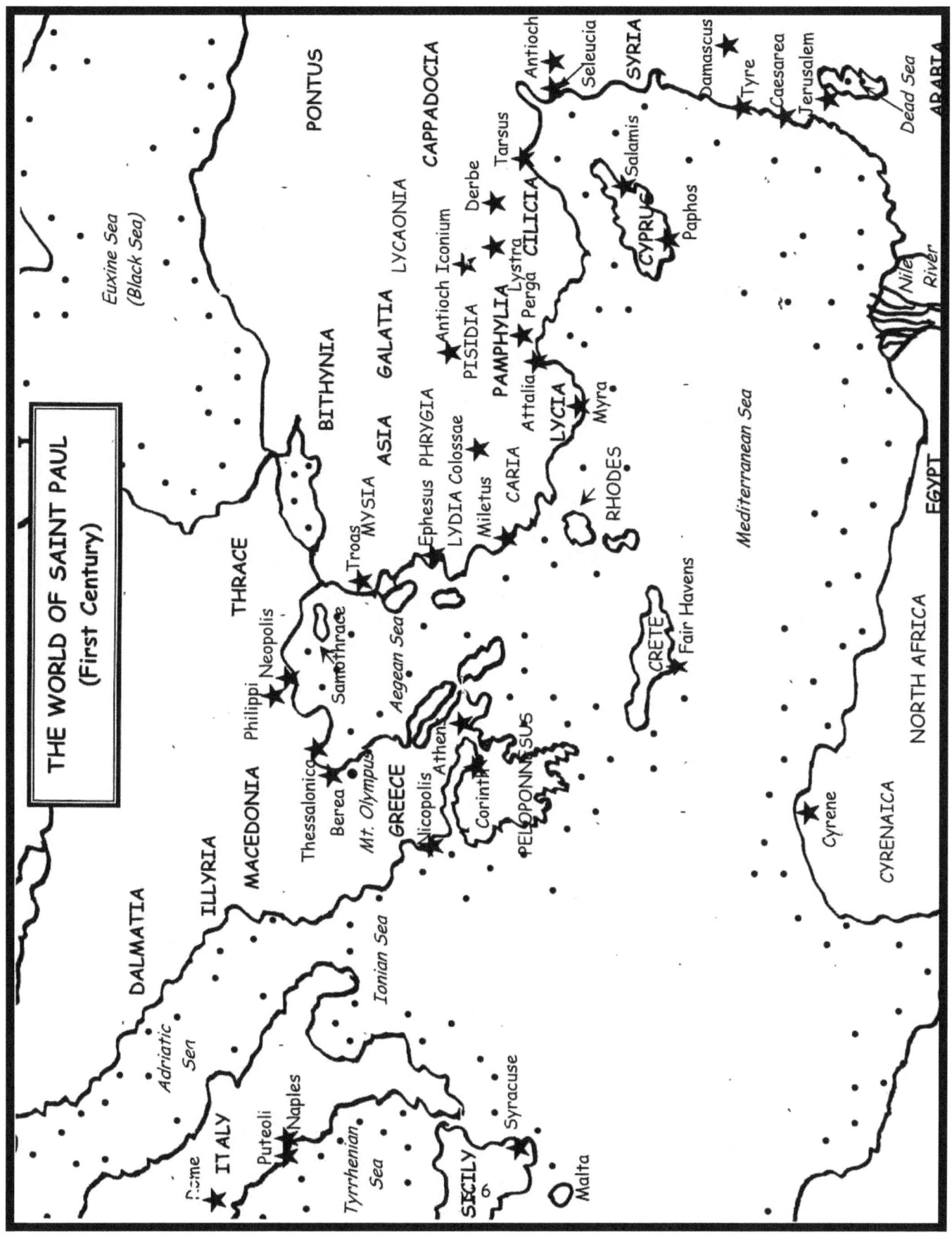

Chapters 1 through 3–In Which Saul Encounters Jesus, Retreats into the Desert, and Begins His Life as a Preacher of the Way

REVIEW Vocabulary

record for *rooting* out the traitors
series of *harrowing* pictures
. . . then so *providentially* disappeared
Saul was outspoken and *impetuous*

Law of Moses (Mosaic Law)
Nazarene(s)
rabbi
prudence

Comprehension Questions/Narration Prompts

Chapter 1
8. Why was Saul traveling to the city of Damascus?
9. What was Saul's "one purpose in life"?
10. What happened to Saul outside the city of Damascus? What does he realize?

Chapter 2
1. How many days did it take for Saul to recover his strength?
2. Who restored Saul's sight?
3. What did Saul then "see"?

Chapter 3
1. What trade did Saul practice while in the desert? Why did Saul fast in the desert?
2. What teachings of Saul caused trouble between him and the Jews as well as between Saul and his fellow Nazarenes?
3. Why did Saul leave Damascus? Where did he decide to go?

Forming Opinions/Drawing Conclusions

1. Based upon your knowledge of Scripture, whose grave was it that Saul and the young soldier passed outside the gates of Damascus?
2. Why did Saul, as a faithful Jew, consider the Nazarenes traitors?
3. What does this expression mean: "It is hard for you to kick against the goad"? (page 4)
4. Why is the title of Chapter 1, "The Pride of Saul," an appropriate title?
5. Saul learns about Jesus—comes to know Him—through his encounter with Jesus on the road to Damascus. What encounters have you had with Jesus? Be more attentive to the moments of grace that God gives you.
6. Name other characters from the Bible who prepared themselves in the desert.
7. Saul is accused of not practicing prudence (page 15). What does this mean? What can you do to become a more prudent person?

For Further Study

1. The Law of Moses—the collection of laws governing the Jewish people—can be found in the first five books of the Bible, the Pentateuch. To better understand the extent of these regulations, (which consisted of 613 different laws), scan the following sections

of the Pentateuch: Exodus 20:1-24:8, Exodus 34:10-35:3, Leviticus 1-7, 11, 19-21, and Deuteronomy 16 and 21-24.
2. On page 128 of this study guide, read "A Brief Overview of the New Testament" which compares the written chronology of St. Paul's letters to their placement in the New Testament canon.

✝ Growing in Holiness

One of the best ways to encounter Jesus—to learn more about Him—is through prayer. St. Francis de Sales believed that we all need to pray at least one-half hour each day—except when we are busy; then we need to pray for an entire hour. Begin to set aside time each day to "go into the desert" of your soul and be alone with the Beloved. As it may be difficult to focus entirely on Jesus for this length of time, use a religious picture book to keep your mind focused on an event in Jesus' life. Feel free to read Scripture—especially the Gospels—during this time also. Read slowly and pause when a phrase inspires you to deeper prayer. In order to be His disciples, we must sit at the feet of the Master and learn from Him. A person of prayer is a person of love.

Geography

Trace the map of the Mediterranean area found on page 91 of this study guide. Label the seas and rivers blue. Label all the areas in capital letters with green. Add the cities of Jerusalem, Damascus, and Tarsus in red lettering. (Additional cities will be added in later lessons.)

✓ Checking the Catechism

1. Older students may review the teaching of the *Catechism of the Catholic Church* (*CCC*) regarding Jesus and the Old Law in text paragraphs 574-582 (113-114) and 1961-1974 (418-421). Read the Church's instruction on the cardinal virtues (especially prudence) in text paragraphs 1780, 1786-89, 1803-09, and 1835 (372, and 377-383).
2. Younger students may study any references to the cardinal virtues and the Bible that may be contained in their own catechisms.
3. Learn more about the Bible by completing Activities #28 and #29 in *100 Activities Based on the Catechism of the Catholic Church* (*100 Activities*).

📖 Searching Scripture

1. Read the first eight chapters of the Acts of the Apostles, which describe the actions of the Nazarenes before the conversion of St. Paul. Then, coordinate the first three chapters of the Windeatt biography with Scripture by reading Acts 9:1-24, and Saul's own description of his conversion in Acts 22:1-16 and Acts 26:12-18.
2. Read the following biblical passages which are referenced in these chapters: Acts 7:54-59(60) (page 2), Matthew 5:17-20 (page 3), Exodus 21:24 (page 10), Matthew 22:34-40 (page 10), Galatians 1:15-17 (page 11), and Acts 9:15 (page 12). Find the passage in the text that relates to each of these Scripture passages.

Saint Paul

Chapters 4 through 7—In Which Saul Travels to Jerusalem, Lives a Life of Prayer, and Accompanies Barnabas to Antioch

 Vocabulary

the *rebuffs* he received
no time to spend in idle *musing*
Saul gave *vent* to his grief
vices of all kinds abounded

Pharisees
synagogue
Gentiles
agape

 Comprehension Questions/Narration Prompts

Chapter 4
1. Although Saul was a "troublesome convert" (page 19), he had an appealing personality. Name several positive traits about the outspoken Saul.
2. How did Saul leave the city of Damascus?
3. How many years after his conversion did he arrive in Jerusalem? What was his reception there? Who was Saul's first friend in Jerusalem?

Chapter 5
1. What work was most dear to Saul's heart?
2. What were the two primary reasons that Saul's message of salvation for all caused such trouble among some of the other Christians?
3. Why did the Christian brethren want Saul to leave Jerusalem?

Chapter 6
1. In a vision at the Jerusalem temple, what commission did the Master give to Saul? What thought consoled Saul as he left Jerusalem?
2. How long did Saul spend in Tarsus praying, studying, and working?
3. Who came to Saul in Tarsus and asked him to journey back to Antioch?
4. What did Saul do to "seek his vocation"?

Chapter 7
1. What was Saul's role in Antioch? By what name were the Nazarenes known there?
2. By what two means does Christ live in us?
3. Why did Saul go to Jerusalem? Who accompanied him back to Antioch?

Forming Opinions/Drawing Conclusions
1. Why do you think Barnabas trusted Saul when others did not? Are you a trusting person, willing to give another a second chance? Is there someone you know who is in need of forgiveness and friendship?
2. Saul had many questions to ask those who had known Jesus personally. What questions might you have asked of Peter and the other disciples?
3. How can you spread the same "glorious message" that Saul preached, "The Messias has come—Jesus Christ of Nazareth!" (page 26)

4. In Tarsus, Saul spent his days working and gave his nights to "studying the Scriptures and to prayer" (page 32). What is the difference between *reading* the Scriptures and *studying* the Scriptures? Which do you do?

 For Further Study

Research first-century Jewish history, culture, language, and religion as well as the relationship between the Jews and the Roman rulers. Define the following terms: Chosen People, the Diaspora, the revolt of the Maccabees, religious feasts, proselyte, Pharisee, Sadducee, Scribe, Zealot, rite of circumcision, Mosiac Law, covenant, and synagogue. How did the "Jews of the Diaspora" and their influence help spread Christianity? What is the difference between a Hebrew, an Israelite, and a Jew?

 Growing in Holiness

Saul gives us lessons in discipleship. He gives Himself entirely to God (page 20). He spends five years learning to know and love the Lord (pages 32-33). Have you experienced Jesus enough in prayer to truly know Him? Saul shows us how to die to ourselves (John 12:24-26) and become like the Master. Read 1 Corinthians 11:1. Do others see Jesus in you?

 Geography

Add these cities to your map: Caesarea, Seleucia, Antioch in Syria, and Cyrene.

 Timeline Work

Taping sheets of plain paper end-to-end, make a timeline representing the years from 44 BC to 95 AD. Let three inches equal 25 years. Mark on your timeline the dates and events from 44 BC through 42 AD, using information from page 90 of this study guide.

 Checking the Catechism

Paul participated in the love feasts or religious suppers with the other Christians to receive the Body and Blood of Jesus (pages 37-38). Review the Eucharist and the history of the Mass in the *CCC* in text paragraphs 1322-58 (271-277) and/or the summary in text paragraphs 1406-19. If desired, complete Activities #52 and #65 in *100 Activities*. Younger students may study the Mass and the Eucharist in their own catechisms.

 Searching Scripture

1. To coordinate these four chapters with Scripture, read the following: Acts 9:25-30, Acts 11:19-30, and Acts 12:25.
2. Read the following biblical passages which are referenced in these chapters: Mark 15:21 (page 36), 1 John 4:7-21 and John 13:31-35 (page 36), John 14:2 (page 37), Galatians 2:19-20 (page 37), and Luke 22:19 (page 37-38).
3. To follow the actions of other first-century Christians, read also Acts 9:31-12:25.

Saint Paul

Chapters 8 through 11–In Which Saul Takes the Name of *Paul* and Begins His First Missionary Journey with Barnabas and Mark

Vocabulary
this man is an *imposter*
a sentence of *banishment*
folk who worshipped *Zeus*
How *contemptible* to be a coward!

vocation
Christian(s)
blasphemy
Master

Comprehension Questions/Narration Prompts
Chapter 8
1. Who did the Church in Antioch choose to lead their missionary work?
2. Why did Saul change his name to the Roman name of Paul?
3. How successful was the missionaries' audience with the Roman governor?

Chapter 9
1. Why did Paul refuse Serguis Paulus' offer to stay at his court in Paphos?
2. Between Attalia and Antioch, what did Mark decide to do?
3. Why did Paul and Barnabas decide to preach only to the Gentiles in Antioch and not to the Jews? What scheme did the Jews decide upon to drive Paul and Barnabas out of the city?

Chapter 10
1. In what ways were preaching to the pagans in Lystra different than preaching to the Jews in Antioch?
2. With whom did Paul and Barnabas stay while in Lystra?
3. What, according to Paul, is the "most glorious thing that can happen to a person"?

Chapter 11
1. Why was Timothy reluctant to give himself "to the Master's service"?
2. How did the Jews from Iconium incite the residents of Lystra to stone Paul?
3. Where did Barnabas and his friends find Paul?

Forming Opinions/Drawing Conclusions
1. What virtues did Saul display when he accepted Barnabas' decision to go to Cyprus—and again when he accepted Barnabas' suggestion that Saul speak before the Roman governor? How successful are you at giving in to others without argument when you disagree with them?
2. Accepting new traditions, new teachings, or any kind of change is difficult. Debate both sides of the issue between Paul and the Jews. Think of a change in rules, routine, or lifestyle within your family or community. How did you (or can you) better accept this new change? Under what circumstances, should new traditions and/or changes be resisted?

3. Do you believe it is easier to preach the Gospel to those whose religious beliefs are completely different from yours or to those whose beliefs are similar? What different strategies would you use for each group?
4. Can you relate to Timothy's reluctance to step out in faith? Have you ever been afraid or reluctant to share your faith in Jesus? Discuss ways to battle this natural reluctance.

 For Further Study

Study the politics, culture, and religion of the Roman Empire. Examine the Roman government (king, republic, empire, emperor, Senate, proconsul, governor, province, and taxes), the Roman army (legion, legionaries, centurion, and cohort), Roman culture (road system, language, clothing, and class structure), and religion (Greek gods, pagans, relationship to the Jewish religion, feasts, temples, and cults). Research the boundaries of the Roman Empire around the time of St. Paul. Read some of the writings of Josephus (37-100 AD), who was a first-century Pharisee and historian.

 Growing in Holiness

". . . when serious matters came up for decision . . . [they] gave themselves to earnest prayer and penance. For a week or more, food and sleep were reduced to a minimum." (page 40) Although prayer and penance should be part of our daily lifestyle, it is especially important in times of decision and discernment. Remember to consult with God on every decision—large and small—that you make.

 Geography

Label in red the following cities: Salamis, Paphos, Attalia, Perga (Perge), Antioch in Pisidia, Iconium, Lystra, and Derbe. Starting in Antioch, connect these cities in order with a purple line to mark Paul's first missionary journey (45-48 AD), ending in Syrian Antioch.

 Checking the Catechism

Discover the *CCC*'s teachings on penance in text paragraphs 1430-39 (300-301) and 2043 (432).

 Searching Scripture

1. To coordinate these four chapters with Scripture, read the following: Acts 13:1-11 (Chapter 8), Acts 13:12-50 (Chapter 9), Acts 13:51-14:18 (Chapter 10), and Acts 14: 19- 20 (Chapter 11).
2. The gift of prophecy (page 40) is a gift not discussed much today. We often think of a prophet as someone who predicts the future. In the first-century, however, this term referred to someone who was God's authorized spokesperson. Read these New Testament references relating to this gift of the Holy Spirit: Romans 12:6-8, 1 Corinthians 12:7-11, and Ephesians 4:11-14.

Chapters 12 through 15–In Which Paul Regains His Strength, Confronts Peter, and Begins His Second Missionary Journey

 Vocabulary

obscure mountain village
obey the *prescriptions* of the Old Law
mystical renewal of the Lord's death
Earnestly they *besought* the Lord

Last Day
Mother Church
Council of Jerusalem
love feast

Comprehension Questions/Narration Prompts

Chapter 12
1. Why did Timothy go with Barnabas and Paul to Derbe?
2. How did Paul make his first convert in Derbe?
3. According to Paul, what is the greatest privilege in the world?

Chapter 13
1. As Paul and Barnabas retraced their steps back to Antioch, what enabled them to better organize the Christian colonies without fear of persecution? How many colonies had they formed?
2. What did the Christians from Jerusalem believe about the Gentiles' share in the heavenly kingdom?
3. What issue did the Council of Jerusalem settle? Who handed down the decision on behalf of Holy Mother Church?

Chapter 14
1. What prompted Paul to accuse Peter of being a hypocrite?
2. How did Peter react to this public accusation? What was the result of his reaction?
3. As Barnabas and Paul readied themselves for their second missionary journey, what caused the two of them to separate?

Chapter 15
1. Who accompanied Paul as he began his second missionary journey in 50 AD?
2. In what way did Timothy consider himself to have been foolish? For what attitude did Paul rebuke Timothy?
3. Who did the three missionaries meet in Troas, located on the Aegean Sea?

 Forming Opinions/Drawing Conclusions
1. Explain the role suffering plays in the conversion of sinners.
2. "The Lord doesn't need our words and actions, but He does want our love—our hearts and wills" (page 65). How can you apply this maxim for holiness in a practical way?
3. In your own words, tell the events of St. Paul's first missionary journey.
4. Do you think that Paul was correct in confronting Peter publicly for his actions regarding the Gentiles? Do you think Paul was right in refusing to give Mark a se-

cond chance? Explain your answers and reasons. Name a time when you have judged someone else harshly. Were apologies made?
5. Paul lists several virtues of Timothy on page 83. What other qualities of a priest and missionary might you add? Do you possess these qualities?
6. "Because you have taken up the Cross, sorrow—the real despairing kind—can never touch you now" (page 83). What does this expression mean?

 For Further Study

The Council of Jerusalem was the first Church council. However, it was not a true general council as only part of the hierarchy participated. Research the twenty-one general Church councils beginning with the Council of Nicea (325) and ending with the Second Vatican Council (1962-1965). Briefly state the primary issues of each council.

 Growing in Holiness

1. Like Timothy (pages 59 and 84), we all grow in trust and holiness by jerks and spurts—sometimes one step forward and two steps back. Do not get discouraged in your spiritual journey. Becoming a faithful follower is not accomplished in a single leap but can be achieved with many small steps. Persevere in your quest for holiness!
2. Peter considered the words of Paul to be "those of the Holy Spirit speaking through him" (page 77). Consider carefully the words others speak to you.

 Geography

Label in red the cities of Ephesus and Troas. Trace in orange the beginning of Paul's second missionary trip from Syrian Antioch to Derbe and Iconium, then across the Galatian and Phrygian provinces to Troas.

✓ **Checking the Catechism**

Older students should learn the teaching of the *CCC* regarding the episcopal college and the ecumenical councils by reading text paragraphs 880-92 (182-187).

 Searching Scripture

1. To coordinate these four chapters with Scripture, read Acts 14:21-15:31 and Galatians 2:1-10 (Chapters 12 and 13), Acts 15:32-38 and Galatians 2:11-14 (Chapter 14), and Acts 15:39-16:8 (Chapter 15).
2. Read the following biblical passages which are referenced in Chapters 12 through 15: Matthew 18:1-4 (page 65), Sirach 35:10 (Ecclesiasticus 35:13) and Matthew 19:27-29 (page 83), and Matthew 6:34 and 1 Corinthians 10:13 (page 84).
3. Read the following Bible passages written by St. Paul on suffering and weakness: Romans 8:18, 2 Corinthians 11:24-30 and 12:9-10, Galatians 6:14, Philippians 1:29-30, and Colossians 1:24.

Saint Paul 101

Chapters 16 through 19–In Which Paul Continues to Be Persecuted in His Second Missionary Journey

 Vocabulary

dragged Paul . . . before the *magistrates*
destroy the world with . . . *tempest*
small *textile* factory
looking for this or that *novelty*

True Faith
fortune telling
Sabbath
idolatry

??? Comprehension Questions/Narration Prompts

Chapter 16
1. What reasons did Luke have for making Lydia's house their headquarters in Philippi?
2. What did Paul do to expel the devil from the fortune-telling slave?
3. How did the owners of the slave react to this exorcism?

Chapter 17
1. For what intention did Paul and Silas suffer their cruel punishment without complaint?
2. Why did Paul and Silas begin to sing the praises of God from the lower prison of Philippi? What happened because of their singing?
3. What information did Paul give the warden that astounded him? What did this information mean for the magistrates who had ordered Paul and Silas to be beaten and imprisoned?

Chapter 18
1. What did Paul and Silas request of the magistrates to provide them with an opportunity to make up for their "terrible mistake"? (page 98)
2. While the others left for Thessalonica, which of the four missionaries stayed behind in Philippi? For what purpose did he stay?
3. In Thessalonica, who was open to the message that the Messiah had already come when it was presented to them by Paul in the synagogue? Who was not open to this message? What accounts for the difference in their reception?

Chapter 19
1. Where did the three missionaries go after narrowly escaping arrest in Thessalonica?
2. What was Paul's experience in Athens? What virtue did he find lacking there?
3. What did Paul find in Athens that washed away his loneliness and misery?

 Forming Opinions/Drawing Conclusions
1. The incident of the slave who told fortunes illustrates the supernatural powers of the devil. What are some ways to tell if supernatural powers come from God or from the devil? Read Matthew 7:15-20.

2. How would you respond to the guard's question on what he must do to be saved? Support your answer with Scripture and the doctrine of the Church.
3. Why did Paul and Silas not tell the magistrates that they were Roman citizens when they were accused? Would you have had the courage—and the faith—to make a similar decision?
4. What virtues did Paul, Silas, and Timothy display in their willingness to work for their food and lodging at each place that they stayed?
5. Why do you think that Silas and Timothy were considered safe in Berea, but Paul was urged to take refuge in Athens?
6. Paul accused the people of Athens of seeking novelty, "They don't care whether a teaching is true or not—they only care whether it's *new*" (page 106). In what ways is our current society guilty of this same accusation? Can the same be said about you?

 Growing in Holiness

While alone in Athens, Paul missed his Christian companions. Read Romans 1:11-12. We need the companionship and encouragement of our fellow Christians. Be sure to cultivate friendships with those who are willing and able to strengthen your faith. Actively encourage others in their faith journey. Help others (especially your family) get to heaven. Become more comfortable talking about Jesus and the virtuous life by increasing each day the number of times you openly talk to others about these topics. Learn to speak openly to others about your faith. Be a proud and vocal Christian!

 Geography

Label in red the following cities on your map: Samothrace, Neopolis, Philippi, Thessalonica, Berea, and Athens. Connect these cities with an orange line from Troas to continue Paul's second missionary journey through present-day Turkey and Greece. Label Mount Olympus brown.

 Timeline Work

Add the dates and events from 44 AD through 52 AD to your timeline.

 Checking the Catechism

The prison warden asked Paul and Silas what he must do to be saved (page 95). Older students may read the teachings of the *CCC* on this issue in the following text paragraphs: 95, 816, 851, 980, 1129, 1257, 1696, 1811, 1816, 2036, and 2744 (17, 162, 239, 1257, and 430).

 Searching Scripture

1. To coordinate these chapters with Acts, read 16:9-22 (Chapter 16), 16:23-37 (Chapter 17), 16:38-17:9 (Chapter 18), and 17:10-21 (Chapter 19).
2. Read the following biblical passages which are referenced in Chapters 16 through 19: Matthew 5:10, Matthew 23:34, Luke 6:27-28, and Acts 7:60 (59) (page 93); and Psalm 103 (102) (page 94).

Saint Paul

Chapters 20 through 23–In Which Paul Completes His Second Missionary Journey, Rests in Syrian Antioch, and Begins His Third Missionary Journey

 Vocabulary

sheet of *papyrus*
to give Paul a *haven*
wonders being *wrought*
Had become *fervent* Christians

Day of Judgment
diocese
New Testament
Apostle(s)

??? Comprehension Questions/Narration Prompts

Chapter 20
1. Why was Paul not very successful in making converts in Athens? Why was he anxious to succeed in Corinth?
2. With whom did Paul stay while in Corinth? What work did he do with them?
3. Why did Paul decide to write a letter to the Thessalonian Christians?

Chapter 21
1. What happened when Paul was brought before Gallio in Corinth?
2. Why did Paul leave Corinth? Who went with him?
3. What was Paul's reception in Jerusalem? In Antioch?

Chapter 22
1. After resting in Antioch for the winter, where did Paul, Timothy, and Titus go to begin Paul's third missionary journey?
2. Whose disciples did Paul encounter in Ephesus? What message did he give them? What gifts did God give to these disciples?
3. What power did God give Paul to help him convert the citizens of Ephesus?

Chapter 23
1. Which of his letters did Paul write from Ephesus?
2. Which virtue did Paul believe the brethren were lacking in Corinth, causing many of the problems in the Church there?
3. What happened when Paul tried to convert the goddess Diana's followers?

 Forming Opinions/Drawing Conclusions
1. Read Paul's first letter to the Thessalonians. How does he address the Thessalonicans' concerns regarding the end of the world and the resurrection of the dead?
2. Consulting a map, explain why Paul went to Jerusalem by way of Ephesus and Caesarea.
3. Explain did John the Baptist's baptisms differ from those performed by Paul?
4. Through Confirmation, God gave the disciples of John the Baptist the gifts of tongues and of prophecy. We too receive many spiritual gifts when we receive the Sacrament of Confirmation. However, many people do not make use of these gifts. Discuss the idea that God's gifts become gifts not when He gives them, but when we open them up.

For Further Study

Research the Greek goddess Diana whose temple was one of the seven wonders of the world. (What were the other six?) Who built the temple and when? When was it destroyed? Who were Diana's father and twin brother? Over what was she the patron, the guardian, and the protector? Preparing graphics, present your research to your family and/or friends in an oral presentation.

 Growing in Holiness

"Oh, if only people everywhere could know Him, could see the reward awaiting those who tried to do His Will. . . . " (page 115). If we truly understood how much Jesus loves us, we would all be saints. However, in order to understand His love and be transformed by it, we need to spend time in prayer. Love does transform. Tell the people you love that you love them—and tell them often. Read and meditate upon 1 John 4:7-21.

 Geography

Label in red the city of Corinth. Complete Paul's second missionary journey by connecting the following cities with an orange line: Athens, Corinth, Ephesus, Caesarea, Jerusalem, and Syrian Antioch. To represent the beginning of Paul's third missionary journey, connect with a green line: Syrian Antioch, Derbe, Lystra, Iconium, Antioch in Pisida, and Ephesus.

 Checking the Catechism

Younger children should review the Sacrament of Baptism in their catechisms. If desired, complete Activities #10 in *100 Activities*.

Searching Scripture

1. To coordinate these chapters with Scripture, read Acts 17:22-18:5 (Chapter 20), Acts 18:6-22 (Chapter 21), Acts 18:23-19:20 (Chapter 22), and Acts 19:21-27 (Chapter 23).
2. Read the following biblical passages which are referenced in Chapters 20 through 23: John 5:28-29 and 1 Corinthians 15:42-58 (page 109); and Mark 1:2-11, Luke 7:18-35, John 1:19-42, and John 3:22-30 (page 121).
3. Read Paul's second letter to the Thessalonians. Paul's letters to the Thessalonians teach us not to worry about the end of the world or even about tomorrow.
4. Read Paul's letter to the Galatians paying special attention to Chapters 5 and 6 which deal with Christian living.
5. Read Paul's first letter to the Corinthians (which may have been his second as it is believed that the first letter was not preserved—See 1 Corinthians 5:9). Read especially 1:10-25 on the divisions in the Church, 11:23-26 on the institution of the Eucharist, 12:12-13:13 on the Body of Christ and Paul's thoughts on the virtue of love, and 15:1-28 on the reality of the Resurrection. We learn from Paul's first letter to the Corinthians that the Church was never perfect.

Saint Paul

Chapters 24 through 27–In Which Paul Completes His Third Missionary Journey and Is Arrested in Jerusalem

REVIEW Vocabulary

Paul *belittles* our goddess
stifling his *anguish*
with every *fiber* of their beings
died away to a *sullen* murmur

bishop
Holy City
Pentecost (Feast of)
Temple

Comprehension Questions/Narration Prompts

Chapter 24
1. What arguments regarding Diana and her temple did Demetrius use in his attempt to get the citizens of Ephesus to turn against Paul?
2. While Demetrius had been going about Ephesus "stirring up serious trouble for Paul" (page 130), what had Paul been doing?
3. What fate did Paul fear had befallen his friends Aristarchus and Gaius?

Chapter 25
1. How was the incident involving Aristarchus and Gaius in the amphitheater resolved? What did Paul decide to do because of this incident?
2. What news did Titus bring to Paul that greatly cheered him?
3. About what topic did Paul speak to his fellow Christians in Troas before leaving them?

Chapter 26
1. What happened to Eutychus while Paul was speaking from the third-story room?
2. What had Paul learned in prayer about what awaited him in Jerusalem?
3. Why was it so difficult for Paul to say goodbye to the Ephesians?

Chapter 27
1. Where was Paul when his Jerusalem enemies attempted to kill him?
2. Who saved Paul from the angry Jews? What did he order done to Paul?
3. What language did Paul speak to the Romans? To the Jews?

Forming Opinions/Drawing Conclusions

1. Several times Paul was in danger from a mob. Briefly discuss the phenomenon of "mob mentality." Where might you see this in our world today? What can you do to prevent a mob from influencing you?
2. Describe the missionary strategy that Paul used throughout all three of his missionary journeys in Asia Minor.
3. Of what New Testament scene with Jesus does the scene at Miletus remind you? Find this scene with Jesus in the Bible.
4. Consider how difficult it is for us to follow God's Will in our everyday life. Imagine how difficult it would be if you knew that doing so would cause you to suffer greatly

(page 143). What can you do now to prepare yourself in case God should ask you to suffer and/or be persecuted for Him?
5. The titles of two of the past four chapters indicate the anger that Paul incited in others. Why was anger a common reaction to Paul's message?

 For Further Study

Chapters 24 and 25 contain references to the amphitheater in Ephesus which contained seating for 25,000 people (page 132). For what purposes were amphitheaters built? Research a more famous amphitheater, the Roman Colosseum. When was it built? How was it made? How large was it? Who saved the it from complete destruction?

 Growing in Holiness

"[Paul] was determined to accept without complaint whatever trials might come his way" (page 146). Memorize Paul's words in Philippians 2:14. Make a pact with a close friend to gently correct each other's complaints and grumblings. Imitate St. Paul's cheerful acceptance of God's Will in your daily life. Use trials as an opportunity to grow in faith.

 Geography

Label the cities of Miletus and Tyre in red. To complete Paul's third missionary journey, connect the following with a green line: Ephesus, Troas, Neapolis, Philippi, Athens, Corinth, Philippi, Troas, Miletus, the Island of Rhodes, Tyre, Caesarea, and Jerusalem.

 Timeline Work

Add the dates and events from 53 AD through 58 AD to your timeline.

 Searching Scripture

1. To coordinate these chapters with Scripture, read Acts 19:28-32 (Chapter 24), Acts 19:33-20:7 (Chapter 25), Acts 20:8-38 (Chapter 26), and Acts 21:1-22:24 (Chapter 27).
2. Read the following biblical passages which are referenced in Chapters 24 through 27: 1 Corinthians 13:1-3 (page 127), and 1 Corinthians 2:9-10 (page 139). Read too James' insight into acceptance of trials in James 1:2-4.
3. Read Paul's second letter to the Corinthians, written while he was in Ephesus. (Some scholars believe that this letter is actually a combination of three or four of Paul's letters to the Corinthians.) Read especially 2 Corinthians 11:16-12:10 which allows us to see Paul as a real human experiencing great suffering as well as ecstatic prayer.
4. Read the letter that Paul wrote while in Corinth to introduce himself to the Romans. Read especially Romans 5:1-14 which contains Paul's theology of justification and salvation, 8:28-39 which expresses Paul's confidence in God's mercy, and Romans 12 which expresses the meaning of Christian life and love.

Saint Paul

Chapters 28 through 31–In Which Paul Suffers Imprisonment for over Two Years—First in Jerusalem, Then in Caesarea

 Vocabulary

was not going to be *hoodwinked*
made an *imperious* gesture
saw clearly through the *flimsy* excuse
Unabashed at so much splendor

Sanhedrin
Sadducees
Old Law

Comprehension Questions/Narration Prompts

Chapter 28
1. Why was the punishment of scourging not carried out on Paul? What was Paul's strategy as he was brought before the Sanhedrin?
2. Who came to Paul "in the safety of his cell" (page 155) to console him?
3. What new plan did the Jews devise in order to murder Paul?

Chapter 29
1. How did Paul leave Jerusalem? Where did he go?
2. What did Paul prophesize about Rome and Jerusalem?
3. What charges did the Sanhedrin bring against Paul in Caesarea? What did the Roman governor (procurator) Antonius Felix decide to do about Paul's case?

Chapter 30
1. Why did Felix refuse to accept the Gospel message that Paul preached to him? How did his refusal affect Paul?
2. What did life in prison do to Paul's health?
3. What happened at Paul's second trial in Caesarea, which was held before the new Roman governor Festus?

Chapter 31
1. What activity delayed Festus' report and the sending of Paul to Rome?
2. What was Paul's response to the order that he entertain the royal visitors?
3. How did Herod Agrippa respond inwardly to Paul's speech? What was his outward reaction?

 Forming Opinions/Drawing Conclusions

1. What did Paul mean when he called Ananias a "whited wall"? (page 154) Read Matthew 23:27.
2. Why was Lysias so concerned about Paul's safety while Paul was under his jurisdiction?
3. Consider why it was so difficult for some of the Jewish people to accept Paul's teachings. Why was it easier for the Gentiles to be more open to the Gospel?
4. Do you believe that Paul made the right decision in appealing to Caesar? Support your argument for or against Paul's decision.

5. Respond to Festus' accusation to Paul, "Much learning has made you mad!" (page 171).
6. Why was King Herod Agrippa "panic-stricken" at the thought of making the standards of Christ his own? Although these are difficult standards, what tools has God given us to make them easier?
7. Can you imagine yourself passionately speaking out about Jesus? Try to be open to opportunities that God may provide for you to be outspoken to others—especially "worldly people"—about Christian values and the rewards of living according to God's standards.

For Further Study
To those living in the Roman Empire in the first century, Roman citizenship was greatly valued. Citizens, like Paul, were given certain privileges. Read more about Roman citizenship on pages 121-122 of this study guide.

Growing in Holiness
Paul feared that the Roman governor Felix and his wife Drusilla "had not even glimpsed the reason for their existence" (page 162). They, like many today, "spent their time in an endless search for happiness" (page 162). Read and meditate on Paul's words in 1 Timothy 6:7-19, which not only tells us how to find true wealth but also implores us to share this message with others. Would Paul have reason to be concerned with how you are living your life? Study Luke 14:33. "Seek yourself in Me" (Teresian motto).

✓ Checking the Catechism
1. Older students may read about our desire for God as the source of true happiness in text paragraphs 27-30, 1035, 1718-19, and 2548-50 (361-362 and 533) in the *CCC*.
2. Study too text paragraphs 520-21, 671-77, 769, and 1816 (133-134) in the *CCC* regarding what persecutions we, as individuals and part of the Body of Christ that is the Church, must endure as we "wait in joyful hope for the coming of our Savior, Jesus Christ."

Searching Scripture
1. To coordinate these four chapters with Scripture, read Acts 22:25-23:18 (Chapter 28), Acts 23:19-24:24 (Chapter 29), Acts 24:25-25:12 (Chapter 30), and Acts 25:13-26:29 (Chapter 31).
2. Read the following biblical passages which are referenced in Chapters 28 through 31: Mark 14:53-61 (page 155), Romans 11:33 (page 161), Genesis 1:26 (page 162), Philippians 3:7-8 and Colossians 3:5-10, (page 163), John 19:28 (page 170), and 1 Corinthians 11:1 (page 172).
3. Read the following New Testament quotations regarding persecution: Matthew 5:11-12 and 10:16-33, John 15:18-22, Acts 5:40-41, Romans 12:12-14, 2 Corinthians 12:9b-10, Philippians 1:29-30, 1 Thessalonians 3:3-4, and 2 Timothy 3:12.

Chapters 32 through 35—In Which Paul Travels as a Prisoner to Rome and Continues His Imprisonment There

 Vocabulary

Despite the *qualms* he had felt
trial before the *imperial* court
ardent Christian life
this *sublime* doctrine

Gospel
convert(s)
Kiss of peace
Mystical Body (of Christ)

Comprehension Questions/Narration Prompts

Chapter 32
1. What arrangements did Festus make for Paul's voyage to Italy?
2. Why was travel dangerous this time of year in the Mediterranean Sea? What danger did Paul and the ship he was on encounter? How did Paul react to this danger?
3. What mercy did the Roman officer offer to the prisoners as they approached land?

Chapter 33
1. What incident caused the natives of Malta to believe that Paul was a god?
2. What did Paul do for the Roman officer Publius and his father?
3. What opportunity did Paul get on Malta that he had not had in over two years?

Chapter 34
1. What events caused Julius to become more impressed with Paul? What did he do for Paul when they reached Rome?
2. Why did the Jews of Rome—like many other first-century Jews—have such difficulty accepting Paul's claim that Jesus was the long-awaited Savior?
3. What news did Paul receive from Tychicus about the Church in Ephesus?

Chapter 35
1. What idea did Paul have to explain each person's unique role in the life of the Church? How do sin and good deeds fit into this model?
2. To what city did Paul write a letter even though he had never visited there?
3. How did Paul view his role as bishop?

 Forming Opinions/Drawing Conclusions

1. "... God has given you all these who sail with you" (page 176). Explain this statement.
2. The people of Malta saw divine intervention when the snake did not bite Paul. Name several simple times that God has intervened in your life over the last week. Can co-incidence really be the hand of God?
3. Discuss Tychicus' concern that the death of true family life will negatively affect the children. Relate this topic to our current society.
4. Does Paul's description of a bishop's duties (page 196) fit with your experience of what your bishop does? Review a list of the documents that the American Catholic bishops have written in the last several years to see what issues concern them. Their

Internet site is www.usccb.org; check "Issues and Actions." Discuss this topic with your parish priest.

✝ Growing in Holiness

1. "Heaven was a place of infinite joy because everyone there was united with God's Will!" (page 193) Unite yourself moment to moment with God's Will. Memorize Paul's prayer and make it your own prayer often throughout the day: "Lord, how hard this is.... But if it is what *You* want, then help me to do it *willingly!*" (page 185).
2. Read through Paul's list of gifts in 1 Corinthians 12:28. However, if you believe that you have not been given any of these gifts, serve God in the alternative manner that Paul describes in 1 Corinthians 13:1-13—the way of love.

Geography

Label in red on your map: Myra, Puteoli, Naples, Good Havens (Fair Havens), Island of Malta, Syracuse, and Rome. Draw a black dashed line from Caesarea to Myra and through the remaining sites to show Paul's trip to Rome.

✓ Checking the Catechism

An original theme of Paul's theology of the Church is that of the Church as Christ's Body. Older students may read about the Mystical Body of Christ in the *CCC* in text paragraphs 774, 787-96, 805-07, and 1396 (156-158). Younger students may review the Mystical Body of Christ and the marks of the Church in their own catechisms.

📖 Searching Scripture

1. To coordinate these chapters with Scripture, read Acts 26:30-27:44 (Chapter 32), Acts 28:1-9 (Chapter 33), Acts 28:10-29 (Chapter 34), and Acts 28:30-31 (Chapter 35).
2. Read the following biblical passages as referenced in Chapters 32 through 35: Matthew 10:1 and Luke 6:19 (page 184), Isaiah (Isaias) 6:9-10 (page 190), and 1 Corinthians 12:27-31 (page 193).
3. Read about St. Paul's idea of the Church as the Mystical Body of Christ in the following passages: Romans 12:4-8; 1 Corinthians 10:16-17 and 12:12-27; Ephesus 1:22-23, 4:1-6, 5:21-30; and Colossians 1:18.
4. Read Paul's letter to the Ephesians, written while he was in Rome. Consider especially the following passages: 3:14-21, Paul's prayer for all; and 5:1-6:4, which contains advice for holy living and Christlike family relationships. In Ephesians, Paul describes the Church as one (4:4-6), holy (5:25-27), catholic (Chapter 2), and apostolic (2:20).
5. Read St. Paul's letter to the Colossians, especially 3:1-21 which outlines the ideal Christian life in the world. Paul's letter to the Colossians encourages us to conquer our sinful habits (3:5-9) and love our neighbor (3:13-14).

Chapters 36 through 39 – In Which Paul Is Freed in Rome and Begins to Travel as a Missionary Again

 Vocabulary

signifying that he was a *fugitive*
began to speak . . . so *eloquently*
count them as *dung*
this would count as partial *atonement*

pagan
brethren
Ascension (Feast of the)
peace of Christ

 Comprehension Questions/Narration Prompts

Chapter 36
1. Who came to Paul for help because he had stolen money from his master?
2. What did Paul suggest that he do?
3. What did Paul believe to be "the first step toward becoming a Christian"?

Chapter 37
1. What did Onesimus decide to do? How did Paul help him?
2. What did Epaphroditus bring Paul from Philippi? How did Paul respond?
3. Who accompanied Peter on his missionary journeys? To whom was Paul remorseful about his "hasty judgment"?

Chapter 38
1. How did Paul's letter to the Philippians differ from his other letters?
2. What happened to delay the delivery of Paul's letter to the Philippians?
3. What was Paul's secret of happiness in this world? (page 209)

Chapter 39
1. When and why was Paul freed from house arrest in Rome? Where did he go upon his release? How long did he stay? Who did he leave in charge?
2. How were the letters Paul wrote to the Christian communities used?
3. What prompted Paul's return to Rome?

Forming Opinions/Drawing Conclusions
1. "There is Someone so rich that He wants to buy every slave in the world" (page 200). Explain.
2. Although neither Peter nor Paul is credited with writing any of the Gospels, which one best corresponds to each of these men? (Hint: Who were their close companions?)
3. ". . . worldly things meant nothing" to him (page 209). How many of us today can make this claim? How can we achieve this high Christian standard?

 For Further Study
1. As this book was written in 1949, Ms. Windeatt did not have access to all of the archeological and historical records that are available to us today. Research (in a

Catholic encyclopedia, the introductory materials to each Gospel in your Bible, or on the Internet) the four Gospels to discover the identity of each author, the purpose for which each Gospel was written, and the approximate date each was written. Write a brief report or prepare an outline with the results of your research.
2. Review each of St. Paul's letters according to the following pattern: *greeting*, naming the writer of the letter and the recipient; *prayer*, usually praise and thanksgiving; *body* of the letter in which he addresses his concerns and explains certain points of doctrine; and the extension of *greetings* to others with a *closing prayer* and *farewell*.

✝ Growing in Holiness

1. "'He just does his part, and leaves the rest to God'" (page 209). Remember to do what you perceive God's Will for you to be. You are responsible for fulfilling your unique role in the Mystical Body. Give God your best efforts, and leave the determination of success or failure to God.
2. ". . . he would be called upon to render an exact account of what he had done with [his time]" (page 215). Guard wisely the use of your time. Review what activities take up your time. Take seriously the necessity of rendering an account for it.

 Geography

On your map, label in red the city of Colossae as a reference point.

📖 Searching Scripture

1. Paul's journey with Titus to Crete in Chapter 39 is recorded in Paul's later letter to Titus, 1:5. Read other references to Titus: 2 Corinthians 2:12-13, 7:6-7, and 8:16-24; Galatians 2:1; and 2 Timothy 4:10.
2. Read these biblical passages which are referenced in Chapters 36 through 39: Philippians 1:3-4 (page 207), Philippians 1:20-24 (page 208), Philippians 3:7-8 and 3:14 (page 209), Philippians 4:4-7 (page 211), and Hebrews 13:10 (page 213).
3. Read Paul's letter to Philemon. Paul's shortest letter, it contains the powerful message that we are to love all others. Notice that Paul does not address the issue of slavery. First-century Christians realized that they could not change Roman laws. They believed that Christ would soon return, so active social reform was not a priority for them.
4. Study Paul's letter to the Philippians. Modern scholars suspect that this letter, as we know it today, may contain parts of three letters which were later edited into one work. Read especially 2:1-18, a call to live in love and humility; and 4:4-9, which instructs us to live in joy and peace. From this letter of St. Paul, we can discover patterns for Christian living and the Philippian model of community life.
5. Scan the book of Hebrews. Current Scripture scholars do not believe that Paul wrote this book (which is actually a sermon, not a letter) as the language and style are so different from Paul's other works. Note the lack of a greeting in Chapter 1(1:1-4). Research the authorship if desired. (See also page 128 of this study guide.)

Chapters 40 through 43–In Which Paul Endures Hardship and Is Martyred for the Faith

---

REVIEW Vocabulary

escaped Nero's *wrath*
certain *leniency* in the treatment
instructing him, *admonishing* him
reprove, entreat, *rebuke*

heretics
martyrdom
Communion of Saints
grace(s)

??? Comprehension Questions/Narration Prompts

Chapter 40
1. Why did Paul leave Rome? Where did he go?
2. Why did Paul write his first letter to Timothy in the summer of the year 66?
3. To whom did Paul write his second pastoral letter?

Chapter 41
1. In the spring of 67, what conditions did Paul and Luke find in Rome for the Christians? What other notable Christian was also in Rome at that time?
2. On what charge was Paul arrested? Into which prison was he housed?
3. Describe the hardships Paul endured in this Roman prison. To whom did he write, "instructing him, admonishing him, and urging him to come" (pages 224-25)?

Chapter 42
1. Why did Paul wish his friend to come quickly?
2. Who did Paul commend for coming to visit him in his Roman prison?
3. Why were Paul's friends afraid after they visited him? What news alarmed Paul?

Chapter 43
1. Why did Paul's sufferings—his cold, hunger, and loneliness—no longer seem important? What was now important?
2. What type of death did Peter suffer?
3. When, where, and how was Paul killed?

 Forming Opinions/Drawing Conclusions
1. Why do you think Paul was so determined to go to Rome?
2. Discuss this quotation from the second-century apologist Tertullian: "We [Christians] multiply whenever we are mown down by you; the blood of Christians is seed."
3. Compare and contrast the two types of prisons that housed Paul in Rome—the first from 61 to 63 and the second beginning in 67.
4. Explain how Paul's death was "just the beginning of victory" (page 231).

 For Further Study
Review the remaining books of the New Testament: the seven "catholic letters"—all addressed to the universal church—and Revelation which is full of symbolic language.

✝ Growing in Holiness

"He continued to praise the Lord" (page 224). Very often, our prayers are prayers of petition. Remember how Paul, while enduring great suffering and loneliness in prison, took time to praise the Lord. Spend some quiet time each day in praise. Compose a simple prayer of praise, and recite this prayer frequently throughout the day. Like Paul in prison, praise Him with song!

Geography

Label in red the city of Nicopolis to complete your map.

Timeline Work

Add the dates and events from 53 AD through 95 AD to complete your timeline.

✓ Checking the Catechism

1. Older students may read text paragraphs 852, 946-948, 954-962, 1173, 2113, 2471-74, 2635, and 2684 in the *CCC* regarding martyrs (173, 234, 262, and 522) and the communion of saints (194-195, 211).
2. Younger students may study their catechisms' teachings on the communion of saints as well as the various types and methods of prayer. If desired, complete Activities #1, "I Believe in God the Father . . ." and #3, "I Believe in Jesus Christ" in *100 Activities*.

📖 Searching Scripture

1. Read the following biblical passages which are referenced in Chapters 40 through 43: 1 Timothy 1:3 (page 219), Matthew 28:20b (page 222), Matthew 16:18 (page 222), 2 Timothy 4:9 (10) (page 224), 2 Timothy 4:9-11 (page 226), 2 Timothy 1:16-18 (page 226), 2 Timothy 4:2-5 (page 227), and 2 Timothy 4:6-8 (page 227).
2. Paul wrote the first of his pastoral letters (letters that deal with issues that concern pastors such as correct doctrine and church organization) to Timothy, one of Paul's most trusted associates. Read 1 Timothy paying particular attention to Chapter 1, which cautions against vices and false teaching; and Chapter 3, which outlines the qualifications of bishops and deacons. 1 Timothy teaches us the value of organization for unity and the importance of opposing false doctrine.
3. Read Paul's pastoral letter to Titus, which shows us the leadership problems faced by the early Church as well as instructing us on how to live Christlike lives in the midst of an imperfect world—Titus 2:1-3:7.
4. In his second letter to Timothy, Paul is pessimistic about the outcome of his case. He relates the trials he is undergoing in the Roman prison and asks Timothy to visit him. He speaks of his approaching death with confidence and inspires us to face the future with hope. He solemnly charges Timothy to be faithful to the Gospel. We learn of the trials endured by the first missionaries and the dangers of false doctrine.

Book Summary Test for *Saint Paul the Apostle*

Directions: Answer in complete sentences. If necessary, use the back of the page for additional writing space. 100 possible points, 20 points for each answer.

1. When and where was St. Paul born? What was his religious background? As this story started, what was his "one purpose in life"? By what other name was St. Paul known? Explain.

   _____

   _____

2. Relate the incident of St. Paul's conversion.

   _____

   _____

   _____

3. How many missionary trips did St. Paul make? Name some of his companions and the general areas that he visited.

   _____

   _____

   _____

4. Relate the types of persecution St. Paul endured. Names at least five books of the Bible that he wrote. Give the date and circumstances of his death.

   _____

   _____

   _____

5. How did the story of St. Paul's life inspire you? What have you resolved to do differently after studying St. Paul's life?

   _____

   _____

Saint Paul the Apostle, The Story of the Apostle to the Gentiles
Answer Key to Comprehension Questions

Chapters 1 through 3—In Which Saul Encounters Jesus, Retreats into the Desert, and Begins His Life as a Preacher of the Way

Chapter 1
1. Saul was traveling to the city of Damascus to rout out the followers of Jesus of Nazareth. He believed that these sect members were betrayers of the Law of Moses and deserved to die a slow death.
2. Saul's "one purpose in life" was to destroy the followers of the Nazarene.
3. Outside the city of Damascus, Saul encountered Jesus as a flash of light knocked him to the ground. Jesus asked him why he was persecuting Him. Jesus told Saul to go into the city of Damascus where he would be told what to do. This encounter left Saul blind. He realized that the Messiah had already come—and he had been persecuting His followers.

Chapter 2
1. Saul was weak, sick, and blind for three days before he recovered his sight and his strength.
2. The Lord Jesus through the hands of Ananias restored Saul's sight.
3. After he recovered his strength and eyesight, Saul could see with the eyes of the Spirit that salvation did not lie in the hundreds of "do's" and "don'ts" of the Old Law but in the New Law as taught by Jesus Christ of Nazareth. He was baptized in the Barada River and became a Nazarene himself. (Note: Almost immediately after Jesus' resurrection, the Christians initiated new members with Baptism. Along with the "breaking of bread" [Eucharist], baptism was a distinguishing feature of the New Way.)

Chapter 3
1. While in the desert, Saul led a holy life and supported himself by making tents, "supplying the desert caravans with a variety of strong, weather-proof tents which he had woven out of black goats' hair upon his portable loom" (page 12). In the desert, Saul practiced penance—particularly fasting—"so that his soul might become purified and more attuned to the voice of God. . . . his heart was not completely emptied of self. . . . he must bend all his energies to accomplish this, so that he might more readily be guided by the promptings of grace" (page 13).
2. Saul's teaching that Jesus Christ came to save all men—Jews, Gentiles, saints, sinners, black, white—caused trouble between him and the Jews as well as his fellow Nazarenes. The Jews had been trained to look upon the Gentiles as unclean, and his fellow Nazarenes were opposed to him speaking out so plainly. They were also opposed to Saul's preaching against the Law of Moses.
3. Saul left Damascus as he learned of a plot to kill him. He did not believe that God wished him to die a martyr's death yet as there was "too much work to be done" (page 17). Therefore, Saul decided to go to Jerusalem.

Chapters 4 through 7— In Which Saul Travels to Jerusalem, Lives a Life of Prayer, and Accompanies Barnabas to Antioch

Chapter 4
1. Several positive traits about the outspoken Saul include his "eagerness to serve, his fiery zeal for truth, his enormous knowledge of the Law and of the Prophets—above all, his love for the One he had persecuted" (page 19).
2. Saul left the city of Damascus in a merchant's basket. He was carried in the basket from his house to a house built into the wall of the city. He was then lowered from a window to the ground. Afterwards, he traveled by foot to Jerusalem—a journey of about 150 miles.

3. Four years after his conversion to the Faith, Saul arrived in Jerusalem. He received a hostile reception there as the other Christians did not believe he had truly converted. They were afraid that he would trick them and continue to persecute them. After some time, Barnabas befriended Saul and introduced him to Peter, James, and the other Christians in Jerusalem.

Chapter 5
1. The work most dear to Saul's heart was "that of preaching Christ and His Gospel" (page 26).
2. The two primary reasons that Saul's message of salvation for all caused such trouble among some of the other Christians was that the other Christians "had sought their converts chiefly from among the Jewish people, and had made few if any comparisons between the Old Law and the New" (page 27).
3. The Christian brethren insisted that Saul leave Jerusalem as his life was in danger. Although Saul was willing to suffer martyrdom, they feared that his death would start another general persecution of Christians just as Stephen's death had done. (See Acts 8:1 and Acts 11:19.)

Chapter 6
1. In a vision at the Jerusalem temple, Jesus told Saul, "Go, for unto the Gentiles afar off will I send you" (page 30). The thought that the Lord Himself had commanded him to leave Jerusalem consoled Saul in his departure.
2. Saul spent five years in Tarsus praying, studying, and working; he felt that despite his "great love for the Lord and his eagerness to bring Him souls . . . he was not ready" for such work (page 32).
3. Barnabas came to Saul in Tarsus and asked Saul to journey back with him to Antioch to help Barnabas with the converts there.
4. Saul actively sought his vocation for five years by working during the day and spending nights in prayer and study of the Scriptures. (Remember that the Scripture Saul studied only included the Old Testament—the Torah. For information on Jesus, he had to rely on those who had known Him.)

Chapter 7
1. Saul's initial role in Antioch was that of a helper to Barnabas and the other Christians. He was not yet being called upon to lead. It was in Antioch around this time that the Nazarenes first came to be called Christians.
2. Christ lives in us "first, by reason of Baptism. Second, by reason of the Holy Eucharist" (page 37).
3. Saul traveled to Jerusalem with Barnabas to bring contributions of "money, food, and clothes" (page 38) to the brethren due to the famine there. After several weeks in Jerusalem, Barnabas and Saul returned to Antioch accompanied by Mark, Barnabas' nephew who had known Jesus.

Chapters 8 through 11—In Which Saul Takes the Name of Paul and Begins His First Missionary Journey with Barnabas and Mark

Chapter 8
1. During the peace that followed the death of King Herod Agrippa in 43 AD (Acts 9:31), the Church in Antioch decided to send out missionaries. The elders of the Church chose Saul and Barnabas to lead this important work. Initially, Barnabas' nephew Mark accompanied them.
2. Beginning with his meeting with the Roman governor Sergius Paulus at Paphos, Saul used his Roman name Paul instead of his Hebrew name Saul. He believed that his Roman name would give him more respect with those he was trying to convert, the Gentiles. The use of double names (one Semitic and one Roman) was not unusual at this time for Jews who were also Roman citizens; for example, the disciple not chosen to replace Judas (Acts 1:23) was known as Justus (Roman) and Barsabbas (Semitic). (In Scripture, a change of name often indicates a new status or relationship with God. Can you think of any Old Testament examples of this phenomenon?)
3. The missionaries' audience with the Roman governor Sergius Paulus was very successful in that the governor and his counselors were all ready to renounce their belief in the pagan gods and ask to be baptized. However, the Jewish magician Barjesus was very hostile to Paul's message.

Saint Paul

Chapter 9
1. Paul declined Sergius Paulus' offer to stay in Paphos as he felt called to travel and bring the Gospel message to as many people as possible.
2. At Perga on their way to Antioch, Mark decided to return to Jerusalem as he was homesick. He did not feel called to be a missionary and travel the countryside.
3. Paul and Barnabas' message that Christ had come to save everybody, even those outside the Jewish faith, shocked many of the Jews in Antioch. They could not accept that the Christians were not bound to "observe the ancient Law of Moses" (page 49). The Jews devised a scheme to convince the Romans that Paul and Barnabas were "plotting the downfall of the Empire, and no Roman family in Antioch was safe" (page 50). Their plan worked; the Romans publicly flogged and evicted Paul and Barnabas from the city. (Note that flogging—39 lashes on the back—was a common practice whether one was innocent or guilty.)

Chapter 10
1. Preaching to the pagans in Lystra was different than preaching to the Jews in Antioch in that the Jews were threatened and hostile to their message. The pagans were more open but also superstitious. They misunderstood and believed Paul and Barnabas were gods who had come to them in disguise.
2. While in Lystra, Paul and Barnabas stayed with the elderly Lois, her widowed daughter Eunice, and Eunice's son Timothy.
3. According to Paul, the most glorious thing that can happen to a person is "to work for the Lord, and then to die for Him" (pages 57-58).

Chapter 11
1. Timothy was reluctant to give himself "to the Master's service" (page 59) as he did not wish to leave his family and his comfortable home. He was afraid to live a life of hardship—a life filled with danger and uncertainty.
2. The Jews from Iconium got the residents of Lystra to stone Paul by telling them lies; they told them that Paul had cured the beggar through magic and that Paul was a deceiver who had been banished from every town he had entered.
3. Barnabas and his friends found Paul, badly beaten and barely alive, in a ditch near the city gates of Lystra.

Chapters 12 through 15—In Which Paul Regains His Strength, Confronts Peter, and Begins His Second Missionary Journey

Chapter 12
1. Timothy went with Barnabas and Paul to Derbe as Barnabas felt that "Timothy could be of use as a messenger between Derbe and the places where converts would be made" (page 63). He went with the blessing and encouragement of his grandmother and mother.
2. Paul made his first convert in Derbe in his first venture out after his stoning. He was asked how he had received the scars on his face, and he proceeded to tell the story of his conversion and stoning. The man was "so impressed that he asked if he could be a follower of Jesus Christ, too" (page 67).
3. According to Paul, the greatest privilege in the world is to be a follower of Jesus Christ, Savior of mankind (page 67).

Chapter 13
1. As Paul and Barnabas retraced their steps back to Antioch, the changes in government officials enabled them to better organize the growing Christian colonies without fear of persecution. In four years' time, Paul and Barnabas had established seven Christian communities—Salamis, Paphos, Antioch in Pisidia, Iconium, Lystra, Derbe, and Perge (Perga).
2. The Christians from Jerusalem believed that the Gentiles had a lesser share in the heavenly kingdom—"To the Jews belonged the chief place" (page 71).
3. The Council of Jerusalem, which took place in 49 AD, settled the issue of the Gentile-Christians' obligation to the Old Law. St. Peter, on behalf of Holy Mother Church, decreed at this council that the Gentile-Christian converts did not have to observe the precepts of the

Old Law. There would no longer be a distinction between the Gentile converts and the Jewish-Christian converts.

Chapter 14
1. When Peter came to Antioch and refused to eat at the table of the Gentile-Christians when the Pharisees from Jerusalem were there (after eating with them when the Jewish-Christians from Jerusalem were not there), Paul publicly accused Peter of being a hypocrite.
2. Peter reacted to this accusation by apologizing for his behavior and acknowledging that Paul was right. Peter had not wanted to hurt the Jewish-Christians but realized that his behavior was unfairly hurtful to the Gentile-Christians. As a direct result of this humble apology, scores of Gentiles converted in Antioch as they realized that Christianity produced a "new and genuine brotherhood" (page 78).
3. As Barnabas and Paul readied themselves for their second missionary journey, the two of them argued over whether or not a second chance should be given to Mark, who wished to accompany them. Paul refused to give allow Mark to join them, while Barnabas insisted that Mark be given a second chance. Because of this disagreement, the two missionaries decided to go their separate ways.

Chapter 15
1. As Paul began his second missionary journey in 50 AD, he was accompanied from Antioch by a disciple named Silas. After being ordained to the priesthood by Paul and Silas, Paul's young friend Timothy joined them in their missionary travels.
2. Timothy considered himself to have been foolish in his fear of suffering in the Lord's service. Paul rebuked Timothy for his concern about the future, "The present moment is the important one, Timothy. The Lord wants us to give ourselves to Him here and now. If He does send trials tomorrow, He will send the grace to bear them, too" (page 84).
3. The three missionaries meet Luke the physician in Troas. (Luke later wrote one of the Gospels as well as the Acts of the Apostles. When we read the Acts of the Apostles, it is the words of Luke, Paul's companion, that we read.)

Chapters 16 through 19—In Which Paul Continues to Be Persecuted in His Second Missionary Journey

Chapter 16
1. Luke encouraged Paul to make Lydia's house their headquarters in Philippi as he believed that Lydia and her friends "would benefit by receiving extra instruction" (page 87). He also felt that Lydia's business association with so many highly-important people would provide "plenty of valuable contacts" (page 87) for the missionaries. (Note: In the paragraph after this quotation is a reference to the "love feast" held each Saturday night at Lydia's house. The early Christians offered the Holy Sacrifice each week beginning almost immediately after the Resurrection. As distinguishing themselves from their Jewish heritage was a gradual process, they still considered themselves to be Jews—not a new religion quite yet but Jewish followers of the New Way. For this reason, this celebration took place on the Jewish Sabbath. The dominant place for early Christian worship [preaching, breaking bread, praying] took place in private houses. Early New Testament references to the "church," such as in 1 Corinthians 16:19, Colossians 4:15, and Philemon 2, repeatedly refer to gatherings at an individual's house. This may be the origin of the identification of the Christian community as the "household of God.")
2. Paul expelled the devil from the slave who was being forced to tell fortunes by addressing the evil spirit within her and commanding the spirit to leave the girl in the name of Jesus Christ.
3. The owners of the slave were angry that their slave could no longer see hidden things and predict the future. They dragged Paul and Silas before the local officials and accused them of being traitors. The officials responded by demanding that Paul and Silas be beaten with rods and sent to prison.

Chapter 17
1. Paul and Silas suffered their cruel punishment without complaint with the prayer that God would grant many souls in Philippi to receive the great gift of faith—and that perhaps "Philippi itself would become the cornerstone of the Church in Europe" (page 92).
2. Paul and Silas began singing the praises of God from their prison cell as they were concerned about the moaning and cursing of the other prisoners. They were encouraged to think that even from their prison cell they could still help spread the Gospel message. Because of their singing, God responded with an earthquake that freed them and all the other prisoners. The prison warden was so inspired that he converted to the Faith immediately.
3. To the astonishment of the prison warden, Paul told him that both he and Silas were Roman citizens. This information could have ruined the lives of the magistrates who had ordered Paul and Silas to be beaten and imprisoned, as Roman citizens of the first century received special privileges and were to be treated in a far different manner than other prisoners.

Chapter 18
1. To provide the magistrates an opportunity to make up for their terrible mistake, Paul and Silas requested the following: The officials must clear their name before the people, provide them with an official escort to their own headquarters (Lydia's house), allow them to work in peace, and provide them with another escort to the city gates when Paul and Silas were ready to leave Philippi.
2. While the others left for Thessalonica, Luke stayed behind in Philippi to look after the new church and provide continued instruction to the new converts.
3. The Greeks in the congregation were open to the message that the Messiah had already come when it was presented to them by Paul in the synagogue. However, the Jews themselves felt that this teaching was blasphemy and contrary to their expectations of the long-awaited Messiah, who was expected to come as a king to make Israel the greatest nation in the world. (Note: First-century Jewish-Christians often preached in the synagogue. However, when in a community where less than ten Jewish families resided, no synagogue would be available. For example, in Acts 16:13, Paul preaches on the riverbank outside the city gate of Philippi).

Chapter 19
1. After narrowly escaping arrest in Thessalonica, Paul, Silas, and Timothy crept away under cover of darkness and arrived twelve hours later in Berea at the foot of Mt. Olympus.
2. Paul described the city of Athens as "a city of idolatry," "empty," "dead," "a soulless pile of marble" (page 105-06). He found the people of Athens lacking in hope—"the people were too uninterested to care whether there was a God or gods!" (page 106). Paul longed for the Christian brethren, for their companionship, and their encouragement.
3. After several weeks in Athens, Paul discovered "a marble altar bearing a single inscription: To the Unknown God" (page 107). This discovery filled him with a new and wonderful hope of reaching the people of Athens.

Chapters 20 through 23—In Which Paul Completes His Second Missionary Journey, Rests in Syrian Antioch, and Begins His Third Missionary Journey

Chapter 20
1. Paul was not very successful in making converts in Athens as the people there were worldly and proud. They did not think an outsider could tell them anything. They were only interested in quoting the ancient Greek writers. Paul was anxious to succeed in Corinth, as Corinth was a bustling city with two harbors; those who visited the harbors on business could return home with the Good News.
2. While in Corinth, Paul stayed with Priscilla and her husband Aquila who had just come from Rome. Paul helped Aquila and Priscilla in their tent-making shop.
3. After Timothy and Silas joined Paul in Corinth from Thessalonica, they told him of the problems in the Church there. As Paul was unable to go to Thessalonica due to the danger for him there, he decided to address a letter to them to "answer all their questions and perhaps encourage them to be more active in the Lord's service" (page 111).

Chapter 21
1. When Paul was brought before the Roman governor Gallio in Corinth, Gallio saw no injustice or crime in Paul's activities. He freed Paul and sent his accusers away.
2. Paul left Corinth in order to go to Jerusalem; he wanted to pray in the temple for Gallio in gratitude for his kind treatment. Silas and Timothy accompanied Paul along with Priscilla and Aquila, whose business had not succeeded in Corinth. (Note: The early Jewish-Christians celebrated the Body and Blood of Jesus Christ each week in private houses but also continued to worship in the Jewish synagogues and at the Temple in Jerusalem. The fall of Jerusalem in 70 AD [including the destruction of the Temple], the Christians' expulsion from the synagogues, the Emperor Constantine's conversion, and the Roman Empire's financing of beautiful basilicas all contributed to later Christians worshiping in buildings we now know as churches. It was probably Paul who made the Christian observance a Sunday celebration; see Acts 20:7 and 1 Corinthians 16:2.)
3. Paul's former enemies in Jerusalem still resented his work among the Gentiles and made him unwelcome there. However, Paul and his companions received a royal welcome in Antioch where the Christian brethren asked to hear repeatedly about his journeys and the souls he had reached with the message of Christ.

Chapter 22
1. After resting in Antioch for the winter, Paul, Timothy, and Titus set out for the cities of southern Galatia—Derbe, Lystra, Iconium, and Antioch in Pisida.
2. In Ephesus, Paul encountered disciples of John the Baptist from Egypt. Paul told them about the Holy Spirit and the events of Pentecost. Upon their Baptism and Confirmation, God gave these disciples "the gift of tongues and of prophecy" (page 123).
3. To help him convert the citizens of Ephesus, God gave Paul the gift of miracles whereby he was able to cure the sick and drive out evil spirits.

Chapter 23
1. Paul wrote his letter to the Galatians and his first letter to the Corinthians from Ephesus.
2. Paul believed that the brethren in Corinth were lacking the virtue of love, which led to many problems in the Church there.
3. When Paul tried to convert the followers of the goddess Diana who flocked to her temple in Ephesus, the silversmiths who made their living selling statues of Diana to the pilgrims became angry with Paul and vowed to cause him trouble.

Chapters 24 through 27—In Which Paul Completes His Third Missionary Journey and Is Arrested in Jerusalem

Chapter 24
1. In his attempt to get the citizens of Ephesus to turn against Paul (and save his silversmith business), Demetrius accused Paul of belittling the goddess Diana. He tried to persuade his fellow Ephesians that Paul wanted the temple destroyed, which would result in less people coming into their town.
2. "Paul paid little attention to Demetrius' lies and slander. Recently he had written another letter to the Corinthians" (page 130).
3. Paul's friends Aristarchus and Gaius had been taken to the amphitheater to be thrown to the lions. When Paul heard a roar of voices coming from the amphitheater, he feared that his friends were dead.

Chapter 25
1. The chancellor Alexander spared the lives of Aristarchus and Gaius in the amphitheater. He dispersed the crowds and lectured Demetrius for his behavior. Nevertheless, Paul felt that he must leave Ephesus due to the danger still present.
2. Titus arrived "with word that Paul's last letter to the Corinthians had settled still more of their disputes" (page 136). This news greatly cheered Paul, and he "really became his old self once more" (page 136).
3. In his departing speech, Paul chose to speak to his fellow Christians in Troas about the indescribable joys of heaven.

Chapter 26
1. The boy Eutychus fell asleep in the windowsill while Paul was speaking from the third-story room in Troas. He fell out the window to the ground below. All of the people thought the boy was dead, but Paul "embraced him tenderly" (page 141). Eutychus opened his eyes, shaken but unhurt.
2. Paul had learned in prayer that great suffering from his old enemies awaited him in Jerusalem.
3. Paul had difficulty saying goodbye to the Ephesians as he knew he would never see them again. He also knew that they would suffer at the hands of those who would try to discredit Paul and rob them of the True Faith.

Chapter 27
1. The enemies of Paul cornered him in the Jerusalem Temple on the Feast of Pentecost in 58 AD and attempted to kill him.
2. The Roman commander of the fortress in Jerusalem saved Paul from the angry mob. He ordered his guards to have Paul scourged.
3. Paul spoke Greek, the Roman language of trade and government, to the Roman commander. He then turned to the Jewish crowd and spoke to them in Aramaic, the language of Palestine. (Note that Latin later became the language of imperial Rome while Hebrew was the language of the Old Testament and Judaism.)

Chapters 28 through 31—In Which Paul Suffers Imprisonment for over Two Years— First in Jerusalem, then in Caesarea

Chapter 28
1. Paul's scourging, ordered by the Roman commander, was not carried out as Paul told the guards that he was a Roman citizen. It was strictly against the law to mistreat or punish a Roman citizen without a fair trial. As he was brought before the Sanhedrin for questioning, Paul decided that his best chance of escaping with his life was to provoke an argument between the two factions within the Sanhedrin—the Pharisees and the Sadducees.
2. Jesus Himself appeared to Paul in his cell in Jerusalem to console him. "Be constant. For as you have testified of Me in Jerusalem, so must you also bear witness of Me in Rome" (page 156).
3. As the Jews plotted to murder Paul on his way to the next meeting with the Sanhedrin, Paul instructed his nephew, who had told him about the plot, to go to the Roman commander Lysias with this information.

Chapter 29
1. Paul left Jerusalem under the cover of darkness. The Roman commander gave him "200 foot soldiers, a company of archers, 200 spearmen and 70 horsemen" (page 158) for protection on his way to the Roman governor in Caesarea.
2. Paul prophesized that someday Rome would be blessed for protecting the followers of Jesus Christ. The city of Jerusalem and its people, however, would suffer great sorrow in return for their refusal to accept the Christian teachings.
3. The Sanhedrin brought several severe charges against Paul in Caesarea. They claimed Paul spent his days "stirring up the people and provoking disorders. Second, he preached a new religion that aimed at the downfall of the Roman Empire. Third, he had recently defiled the Temple. On all three counts he deserved the death penalty" (page 159). The Roman governor (procurator) Antonius Felix did not wish to find Paul guilty, but neither did he wish to make enemies of the members of the Sanhedrin. Therefore, he decided to postpone any decision about Paul's case.

Chapter 30
1. Felix refused to accept the Gospel message that Paul preached to him—even though he feared the pains of hell and wanted peace of mind—as he did not want to pay the price of living a life of self-surrender. Paul's inability to convert Felix caused Paul to feel ineffective as an apostle. Luke countered Paul's sense of uselessness by reminding Paul of the value of suffering.

2. The two years that he spent in prison at Caesarea provided Paul, as a Roman citizen, with plenty of rest and good food, which restored his health.
3. At Paul's second trial in Caesarea, held before the new Roman governor Festus, Festus refused to "give a decision in favor of either side" (page 166). Paul, to the dismay of the members of the Sanhedrin, appealed to Caesar, which was his right as a Roman citizen. This action took his case away from the Sanhedrin and away from the Roman governor as well.

Chapter 31
1. The arrival of King Herod Agrippa II and his queen Beatrice delayed Festus' report on Paul and Paul's departure to Rome.
2. "Paul was certainly was not interested in entertaining these famous people, but he was happy at the thought of being able to tell them about the Lord Jesus Christ" (page 169).
3. Inwardly, Herod Agrippa was impressed with Paul's speech. He was panic-stricken at the mere thought of making the standards of Christ his own. But as "It would never do to let the prisoner know that he had made a real impression on a man of the world" (page 171), Herod made light of Paul's words and intentions, saving himself and the other listeners from having to take Paul's words seriously.

Chapters 32 through 35—In Which Paul Travels as a Prisoner to Rome and Continues His Imprisonment There

Chapter 32
1. After Herod Agrippa left, Festus arranged for Paul to leave for Rome. Paul, along with several other prisoners, was to leave Caesarea "on a small ship bound for Myra in Asia Minor. There the group would board another and larger ship bound for Puteoli, a port not far from Naples" (page 173). Luke, Timothy, and Aristarchus would accompany Paul and would be "given every consideration while on board ship—good food, decent quarters and the chance to move about" (page 173) the boat as they pleased.
2. Travel in the Mediterranean Sea from October until February was dangerous as it was the storm season. "[H]eavy storms would be sweeping the Mediterranean" (page 174). As the ship left Good Havens for Phoenix, "a strong, northeasterly wind swept down upon her" (page 175). The storm raged for two weeks. Throughout the storm, Paul was "the only one to remain calm" (page 176).
3. Under the current circumstances with the possibility of escape so large, Roman law provided that all prisoners be killed. Nevertheless, Julius ordered, after glimpsing Paul among the prisoners, that all prisoners be unchained and allowed to fend for themselves.

Chapter 33
1. When Paul picked up a poisonous snake without getting bit, the natives of Malta believed that this extraordinary event showed that Paul was a god who was not able to die.
2. When Paul laid his hands on Publius' father and invoked the name of Jesus, he was cured.
3. While on the Island of Malta (October 60 to February 61), Paul was able to preach the Gospel—something he had not had the opportunity to do for over two years.

Chapter 34
1. The fond farewell that Paul received from the people of Malta astonished Julius. He became even more impressed with Paul in Syracuse when he saw how "Paul's reputation as a preacher and a wonderworker had preceded him" (page 186). Julius really began to understand Paul's importance when a band of Christians walked forty-five miles out of Rome to meet him. His respect for Paul led him to explain to Burrus, the chief of the imperial police in Rome, what a wonderful man Paul was. This information convinced Burrus to allow Paul to live in a private house in Rome (under guard) rather than in the common prison.
2. The Jews of Rome—like many other first-century Jews—had difficulty accepting that Jesus was the long-awaited Savior as He was a common laborer who had died on a cross. (See Galatians 3:13.) They had "been trained since childhood to look for a Saviour who will be rich and powerful" (page 190).

3. Tychicus, "one of Paul's faithful helpers in Ephesus," told Paul that the Church in Ephesus "had become a group of self-centered souls who had no interest in one another's welfare" (page 191). He was concerned that true family life was dying.

Chapter 35
1. In order to explain each person's unique role in the life of the Church, Paul taught about the Mystical Body of Christ as an analogy of Christ's relationship to the Church and to Christians. Paul explained that, as part of that body, each person who commits sin harms the entire Body of the Church, and each person's good deeds profit the entire Church.
2. Paul wrote a letter to the Christians in the Church at Colossae. He himself had never visited there, but a worker from Colossae, Epaphras, came to Paul for advice. Paul's letter to the Colossians was the result of Epaphras' visit.
3. Paul believed that as a bishop, a spiritual shepherd, he "ought to be chiefly concerned with the welfare of his flock—for their sakes spending himself in prayer, in sacrifice, in a study of the Lord, and His ways" (page 196).

Chapters 36 through 39—In Which Paul Is Freed in Rome and Begins to Travel as a Missionary Again

Chapter 36
1. Onesimus, a young runaway slave from Colossae, came to Paul for help because he had stolen money from his master, Philemon.
2. Paul suggested that Onesimus ask God to help him. He spoke to Onesimus about God's great love for him and told him about His Son, Jesus.
3. Paul believed that Onesimus had taken the first step toward becoming a Christian when he announced "his belief in Jesus Christ" (page 201).

Chapter 37
1. After speaking with Paul and living with him for some time, Onesimus decided to accompany Tychicus back to Colossae to "seek out his master and accept whatever punishment might be inflicted upon him" (page 202). Paul helped Onesimus by converting him to Christianity and by writing a heart-felt letter pleading his case to Philemon, his master.
2. From Philippi, Epaphroditus brought Paul a "most generous sum of money . . . [and] various small luxuries which would make his life in prison much easier" (page 203). Paul responded by writing a letter to the Philippians—"his first converts in Europe" (page 203) to express his gratitude and assure them that he was not suffering mistreatment in prison in Rome.
3. Peter was accompanied on many of his missionary trips with Mark (or John Mark), the nephew of Barnabas. It was this same Mark that Paul had hastily judged as unsuitable for missionary work nearly twenty years previously.

Chapter 38
1. Paul's letter to the Philippians was different from his other letters to Christian communities in that there "was no need to scold or reprove the Philippians. They had always been a model group" (page 207).
2. The delivery of Paul's letter to the Philippians was delayed by the duties of Paul's life, and the nearly fatal illness of Epaphroditus who was to deliver the letter.
3. Paul's secret of happiness in this world was that he had already "suffered the loss of all things" (page 209). "He desired nothing but a knowledge and a love of Christ, for himself and for others. As a result, death held no terrors for him."

Chapter 39
1. Paul was freed from house arrest in Rome in June of 63 after two long years of confinement. After finally having the case brought before him, the Roman Emperor Nero showed little interest in Paul's case and released him. Upon his release, Paul and Titus went to the Island of Crete where Paul stayed throughout the summer of 63. Paul put Titus in charge of the work there when he left.
2. The letters Paul wrote to the various Christian communities were "read, studied, memorized and passed from one Christian community to another with the utmost reverence" (page 215).

3. While Paul spent most of the year 64 in Spain, Nero had begun the persecution of Christians in Rome. Nero blamed them for the devastating fire that had destroyed most of the city. Upon hearing this news almost a year later, Paul immediately set out for Rome to help the Christian communities there.

Chapters 40 through 43—In Which Paul Endures Hardship and Is Martyred for the Faith
Chapter 40
1. Paul left Rome at the urging of his fellow Christians. The Roman Empire was actively persecuting Christians throughout Italy. Paul let himself be persuaded to take refuge in Asia Minor, Macedonia, and Greece. He made "hasty trips" to visit the brethren in Ephesus, Troas, Philippi, Corinth, and Nicopolis.
2. Paul wrote his first letter to Timothy in the summer of the year 66 as Timothy had not been feeling well; with Timothy's additional responsibilities as bishop, Paul wanted to relieve some of Timothy's worry. It was a "fatherly letter . . . full of sympathy and encouragement" (page 219). Paul explained Timothy's duties as a bishop and warned him of the danger of false teachers.
3. Paul's letter to Titus, his second pastoral letter, was written to give Titus advice regarding the heretics at Crete.

Chapter 41
1. Upon their arrival in Rome in the spring of 67, Paul and Luke discovered that Rome was a dangerous place for Christians. Christians were being "bitterly persecuted. The better known among them were in constant hiding . . . and there had been mass arrests and executions" (page 221). The Christians who could claim Roman citizenship were not tortured or thrown to the wild beasts, but they could be condemned to death "as surely as anyone else." Being a Christian in Rome at that time was "a major crime" (page 222). Peter was also in the city at that time and "what splendid work he was doing!" (page 222)
2. Paul was arrested on the charge that "three years ago he had plotted the great fire at Rome, directing the labors of his fellow Christians while word was passed about that he was away on one of his preaching trips" (page 223). He was thrown in the Mamertine prison—a "horrible place with its brutal guards, its torture chambers, its dungeons oozing with slime and filth" (page 223).
3. Life in prison was hard. Paul's cell at the Mamertine prison was dirty, dark, and damp; the food was scant; and he was chained to the wall. Many of his friends had deserted him, particularly Demas. He was lonely. "Presently Paul decided to write to Timothy in Ephesus, instructing him, admonishing him, and urging him to come—and quickly" (pages 224-25).

Chapter 42
1. Paul wanted Timothy to come to Rome quickly as he feared that his case may be called at any moment. "Already autumn was approaching, and soon the Mediterranean would be closed to sailing" (page 226).
2. Paul commended Onesiphorus for seeking him out in prison and persuading the guards to "let them visit together" (page 226).
3. After visiting with Paul, his friends were concerned about his health. He had aged greatly during the weeks of his imprisonment and was very weak. Paul was alarmed about Peter's arrest. Peter had been betrayed by "a number of jealous brethren" (page 228). Paul was concerned that Peter, who was not a Roman citizen, was being tortured unmercifully.

Chapter 43
1. Paul's sufferings—his cold, hunger, and loneliness—no longer seemed important as he knew Peter was suffering far more than he. What mattered now was "that Peter and he should spend their remaining hours fruitfully and well" (page 229).
2. As Peter, unlike Paul, was not a Roman citizen, he suffered a death similar to Jesus—crucifixion. (Tradition tells us that St. Peter asked to be crucified upside down as he did not feel worthy to suffer the same death as Jesus. Tradition also has held that Peter and Paul were both executed on the same day in Rome in 67 AD. 1 Peter 5:13 places Peter in Rome ["Babylon"] with Mark at this time.)

3. St. Paul of Tarsus was martyred in 67 AD during the persecution of the Roman Emperor Nero. Tradition places his beheading (a courtesy granted him because of his Roman citizenship) on the Ostian Way, several miles outside the city of Rome. Peter was crucified and buried on what is now known as Vatican Hill.

Answer Key to Book Summary Test

1. St. Paul was born in Tarsus, Cilicia, a province of the Roman Empire. He was raised as a Jew and was educated by the Pharisees in the Law of Moses. He was "as filled with zeal for the Law and the Prophets as the most learned rabbi at the Temple" (page 2). Before his conversion to Christ, Paul's "one purpose in life" was to "destroy the followers of the Nazarene." Saul was St. Paul's Jewish name. Early in his Christian ministry, he began to use his Roman name of Paul; he believed it would give him more credibility with the Gentiles he wished to convert.
2. St. Paul's famous conversion took place on the road to Damascus. He and several others were headed there to find traitors to the Law of Moses and bring them back to Jerusalem for trial. Outside the gates of Damascus, Saul encountered Jesus. A flash of light cut through the sky, and Saul and his men fell to the ground. Jesus spoke to Saul asking him why he was persecuting Him. Saul asked Him who He was and what He wanted Saul to do. Jesus told him to go into the city, where he would be told what to do. Saul, blind and weak, remained in the city for three days until Ananias, a Nazarene, came to Saul. When Ananias touched Saul, the blindness left him. Saul was baptized and began to preach in the synagogue about Jesus and the New Law.
3. St. Paul made three missionary trips. His first trip, begun with Barnabas and Barnabas' nephew Mark in 45, lasted four years and took him to Cyprus and various cities of Asia Minor. His second missionary journey (50-52) was to Asia Minor, Macedonia, and Greece. Silas accompanied Paul on this trip. On his third missionary trip (53-58), St. Paul (along with Timothy and Titus) journeyed to the areas of Asia Minor, Macedonia, Greece, and then to Jerusalem.
4. Many times during his missionary career, St. Paul had to flee a city under the cover of darkness. He was stoned, beaten, and imprisoned for his outspoken beliefs in the Messiah. St. Paul is credited with writing twelve books of the New Testament: Romans, 1 and 2 Corinthians, Galatians, Ephesians, Philippians, Colossians, 1 and 2 Thessalonians, 1 and 2 Timothy, and Titus. In the events leading up to his martyrdom, St. Paul was imprisoned in Rome for two years, and released in the summer of 63. He returned briefly to Rome in 65 but left due to the severity of the persecutions there under the Roman Emperor Nero. He returned in 67 and was arrested shortly thereafter. After spending some time in prison, he was beheaded on the Ostian Way, several miles outside of the city.
5. Answers will vary.

A Brief Overview of the New Testament

Within the last several decades, biblical scholarship has flourished; we know much more about the New Testament writings now than we did when Mary Fabyan Windeatt wrote her biography of St. Paul in 1949. However, a precise chronology of Paul's ministry is still impossible to determine. It is quite certain that Paul's earlier letters (1 and 2 Thessalonians, 1 and 2 Corinthians, and Romans) were written between the years 50 AD and 58 AD—approximately twelve years after Paul's conversion. That places Paul's letters as the first books of the New Testament, written before any of the Gospels.

Within the context of this study guide, we read the letters of St. Paul in the order in which Ms. Windeatt has Paul writing them—a chronological order still accepted by current biblical scholarship. This order, however, is not the order in which these books appear in the New Testament. In the Bible, St. Paul's letters are not placed in chronological order. Rather, they are grouped after the Gospels and the Acts of the Apostles with his letters to communities located before his letters to individuals, longest to shortest—Romans to Thessalonians. The biblical canon has his letters to individuals next from longest to shortest—1 Timothy to Philemon. (The remaining books of the New Testament are arranged from longest to shortest with like authors together, i.e. 1 Peter, 2 Peter, and 1, 2, and 3 John with the Book of Revelation last.)

Paul's letters can be grouped into two categories: Travel letters (1 and 2 Thessalonians, 1 and 2 Corinthians, Galatians, Romans, and 1 Timothy and Titus), and Captivity letters—or those letters written from prison (Philippians, Philemon, Colossians, Ephesians, and 2 Timothy). Notice that Hebrews is not listed in either category. The authorship of this book has been disputed since the second century. The difference in vocabulary and style between Hebrews and the letters attributed to St. Paul has led current biblical scholars to eliminate Paul as the author of this book, although scholars can agree on no other author.

Paul intended his letters to be read aloud within the community. He also wished each community to share their letters with neighboring communities. Read Paul's letters aloud in your family. Share passages that inspire you. Memorize short passages of St. Paul's words so that you may better imitate the "superhero" of apostles—and therefore imitate Christ Himself. (See pages 122-123 of this study guide for more suggestions on specific topics.)

Roman Citizenship

Initially, Roman citizenship was used to distinguish people who lived in Rome from those who came from the outside. Under the Roman Republic (82-27 BC), Roman foreigners could be granted Roman citizenship but usually only for courageous military service. However, under the Roman Empire, these grants of Roman citizenship (*viritane*) to non-Romans (*peregrines*) became more common and could be obtained a number of ways. Citizenship was granted to those who worked for the Roman government as a government official or as a member of the Roman military. (Honorable discharge from the military after twenty-five years of service resulted in a grant of citizenship and the legitimization of a marriage with a foreign woman. These veterans, like other new citizens, then adopted a Roman name.) Citizenship could also be gained by giving supplies or products to a government official. Artistic performers who pleased an emperor, notably Claudius or Nero, were sometimes granted citizenship on the spot. St. Paul's father may have acquired citizenship by sewing tents for government use. Other ways of gaining citizenship include purchasing it or being born into the family of a Roman citizen, as in the case of St. Paul. (See Acts 22:28.)

Finally, citizenship could be extended to all of the free people of a community. This practice was used in the uncivilized west rather than in the Greek east. This was normally introduced at the level of the city and its territory, but sometimes blanket grants were made. For example, Emperor Vespasian (69-79 AD) gave Roman citizenship to all of Spain, recognizing the extent to which nearly three centuries of Roman settlement there had affected the local population. However, this blanketing of citizenship to communities, along with the vast numbers of citizenships obtained through military service, allowed more lower-class citizens the same privileges as the wealthy. As a result, Roman citizenship had lost much of its significance by the late first-century.

In 212 AD, Emperor Caracalla issued an edict granting Roman citizenship to the entire freeborn population of the empire, an act known as the *Constitutio Antoniniana*. Thereafter no distinction was made between Roman and *peregrine*. Roman citizenship no longer meant much in practical terms anyway, as by then the law had come to distinguish not between citizen and non-citizen but between wealthy and poor.

Records of Roman citizenship were kept in Rome. From the time of Claudius (41-54 AD), troops received a special bronze document recording their grant of citizenship. Additionally, Roman citizens had a birth certificate that was registered in their place of birth as well as carried on their person. This was a waxed plate made of metal or wood. However, the Romans were quite skeptical of the reliability of documents as valid proof. Calling on reliable witnesses was more likely to have been how it worked.

The responsibilities of a Roman citizen in St. Paul's time consisted of paying a head tax, speaking the language of the government (Greek), and being available for jury duty. Roman citizenship endowed privileges in three key areas: political (the right to vote and hold a government office), legal (marriage rights, the right to a trial before punishment, the right to appeal to Caesar, and the right of beheading over crucifixion as punishment for crimes), and economic (the right to move freely throughout the empire, to conduct business unhindered, and freedom from paying certain taxes).

The census conducted by Roman Emperor Augustus in 14 AD registered 4,937,000 Roman citizens, up from the 4,063,000 registered in the census of 28 BC. However, in St. Paul's time, there were more Jews than Roman citizens in the Roman Empire. As Augustus wished to make life tolerable for every class in the empire, the strong, central Roman government allowed local independence; therefore, the Jews had their own courts. While Jesus was tried in both the Roman and Jewish courts, St. Paul was able to invoke his privileges of Roman citizenship to avoid the justice system of the Jews. His Roman citizenship also allowed him punishment by beheading rather than crucifixion.

Sources for "Roman Citizenship" include the following:
1. Internet article from BBC, "Beyond the Broadcast – Making History" with quotes from Dr. Alison Cooley
2. Internet article by David and Jane Graves, "The Scroll – Topical Viewer – Books of the Bible – Acts"
3. "Roman Citizenship," class lecture by C.S. MacKay from the University of Alberta, Canada

Quotations from the Letters of St. Paul

"As for his letters, they were read, studied, memorized and passed from one Christian community to another with the utmost reverence" (page 215). Read and study some of the following passages.

Doctrine

Romans 6:3-4 - Baptism
Romans 8:26-27 – Saints
1 Corinthians 2:10-11 – Holy Spirit
1 Corinthians 3:14-15 – Purgatory
1 Corinthians 7:32-34 - Celibacy
1 Corinthians 10:16-17 – Eucharist
1 Corinthians 11:2 - Tradition
1 Corinthians 11:23-32 – Eucharist
1 Corinthians 13:13 - Virtues
2 Corinthians 5:18 – Reconciliation

2 Corinthians 13:13 – Trinity
Galatians 5:22-23 – Fruits of the Spirit
Ephesians 4:30 – Holy Spirit
Ephesians 6:18 - Saints
Colossians 1:24 – Unity with Christ
2 Thessalonians 2:15 – Tradition
1 Timothy 2:1 – Saints
2 Timothy 3:16-17 - Scripture
Titus 3:5 – Baptism

Considerations

Acts 20:24 – Unimportance of life
Romans 5:8 – God's love for sinners
Romans 6:11 – Live for Christ
Romans 6:23 – Wages of Sin
Romans 8:24-25 – Hope
Romans 8:26b – Prayer
Romans 8:31 – Power of God
Romans 8:38-39 – Love of God
1 Corinthians 1:18 – The Cross
1 Corinthians 1:25 – Wisdom/strength
1 Corinthians 3:19a – God's wisdom
1 Corinthians 9:24-27 – Race for Heaven
1 Corinthians 10:13 – Trials

2 Corinthians 5:17 - Made new in Christ
2 Corinthians 11:24-27 – Trials of St. Paul
2 Corinthians 12:9a – Grace and weakness
2 Corinthians 13:5 – Test of faith
Philippians 2:12 – Work out own salvation
Philippians 3:7-8 – Value of worldly things
Philippians 3:17-19 – Wrong conduct
Colossians 3:12-17 – Guidelines for living
1 Thess. 5:14-22 – Christian living
1 Timothy 1:5 – Purpose of instruction
1 Timothy 4:16 – For teachers

Saint Paul

1 Timothy 6:17-19 – Use of wealth
2 Timothy 2:11-13 – Life in Christ
2 Timothy 3:1-5 – End times
2 Timothy 4:2-4 – End times

Christian Living

Memorize several of the following instructions to the early Christians regarding how they should live. Live out these teachings in your daily life.

Acts 20:35b – Unselfishness
Romans 2:1 – Judging others
Romans 2:21a – Teachers' example
Romans 12:1-2 – Will of God
Romans 13:1 – Authority
1 Corinthians 3:7 – Humility
1 Corinthians 6:19-20 – Body as Temple
1 Corinthians 10:31 – Glory of God
1 Corinthians 11:1 – Imitate St. Paul
1 Corinthians 14:40 - Orderliness
1 Corinthians 15:33 – Bad company
1 Corinthians 16:14 – Firm faith
2 Corinthians 3:5 – Credit to God
2 Corinthians 5:7 – Walk by faith
2 Corinthians 9:6-7 – Cheerful giver
2 Corinthians 13:11 – Peaceful living
Galatians 6:9-10 – Do good to others
Ephesians 4:31-32 – Forgiveness
Ephesians 5:4 – Christ-like speech
Ephesians 5:10 – Pleasing God
Ephesians 6:11 & 16-17 – Armor of God
Ephesians 6:18 – Constant prayer
Philippians 2:3-4 – Selfless living
Philippians 2:14 – Cheerfulness
Philippians 4:8 – Worthy thoughts
Colossians 3:2 – Worthy thoughts
Colossians 3:20 – Obey parents
Colossians 4:2 – Prayer
Colossians 4:6 – Gracious speech
1 Thess. 5:11 – Encourage others
1 Thess. 5:17 – Prayer
1 Timothy 4:8 – Physical training
1 Timothy 6:10 – Love of money
2 Timothy 2:16 – Useless talk
2 Timothy 2:23 – Quarrelsome debates
Titus 1:16a – Knowledge vs. deeds

Memorize in order the books of the New Testament. You probably already know the Gospels. Now that you are more familiar with Acts and the letters of St. Paul, you have an excellent start—only eight books left!

Other RACE for Heaven Products

Catholic Study Guides for Mary Fabyan Windeatt's Saint Biography Series teach the Catholic faith to all members of your family. Written with your family's various learning levels in mind, these flexible study guides succeed as stand-alone unit studies or supplements to your regular curriculum. Thirty to sixty minutes per day will allow your family to experience:

- ☑ The spirituality and holy habits of the saints
- ☑ Lively family discussions on important faith topics
- ☑ Increased critical thinking and reading comprehension skills
- ☑ Quality read-aloud time with Catholic "living books"
- ☑ Enhanced knowledge of Catholic doctrine and the Bible
- ☑ History and geography incorporated into saintly literature
- ☑ Writing projects based on secular and Catholic historical events and characters

Purchase these guides individually or in the following grade-level packages. (Grade level is are determined solely on the length of each book in the series.)

Grades 3-4: *St. Thomas Aquinas, The Story of the "Dumb Ox"*; *St. Catherine of Siena, The Girl Who Saw Saints in the Sky*; *Patron Saint of First Communicants, The Story of Blessed Imelda Lambertini*; and *The Miraculous Medal, The Story of Our Lady's Appearances to St. Catherine Labouré*

Grade 5: *St. Rose, First Canonized Saint of the Americas*; *St. Martin de Porres, The Story of the Little Doctor of Lima, Peru*; *King David and His Songs, A Story of the Psalms*; and *Blessed Marie of New France, The Story of the First Missionary Sisters in Canada*

Grade 6: *St. Dominic, Preacher of the Rosary and Founder of the Dominicans*; *St. Benedict, The Story of the Father of the Western Monks*; *The Children of Fatima and Our Lady's Message to the World*; and *St. John Masias, Marvelous Dominican Gate-keeper of Lima, Peru*

Grade 7: *The Little Flower, The Story of St. Therese of the Child Jesus*; *St. Hyacinth, The Story of the Apostle of the North*; *The Curé of Ars, The Story of St. John Vianney, Patron Saint of Parish Priests*; and *St. Louis de Montfort, The Story of Our Lady's Slave*

Grade 8: *Pauline Jaricot, Foundress of the Living Rosary and the Society for the Propagation of Faith*; *St. Francis Solano, Wonder-Worker of the New World and Apostle of Argentina and Peru*; *St. Paul the Apostle, The Story of the Apostle to the Gentiles*; and *St. Margaret Mary, Apostle of the Sacred Heart*

The Windeatt Dictionary: Pre-Vatican II Terms and Catholic Words from Mary Fabyan Windeatt's Saint Biographies explains over 450 Catholic terms and expressions used in this popular saint biography series. Indispensable in expanding knowledge and practice of the Catholic faith, this book provides a ready access for the Catholic vocabulary words used in the RACE for Heaven Windeatt study guides. This dictionary also includes a Catholic book report resource that contains suggestions for forty-five Catholic book reports: fourteen writing projects, ten book report activities, and twenty-one topics for saint biographies.

Graced Encounters with Mary Fabyan Windeatt's Saints: 344 Ways to Imitate the Holy Habits of the Saints is a compilation of the "Growing in Holiness" sections of RACE for Heaven's Catholic study guides for the Windeatt saint biography series and presents 344 examples of saintly behavior, one for nearly every chapter in each of these twenty biographies. Enhance your encounter with the saints by practicing the models of devotion, service, penance, prayer, and virtue offered in this guide.

Bedtime Bible Stories for Catholic Children: Loving Jesus through His Word contains twenty discussions of Bible stories that were originally published in serial form in a Catholic children's magazine. Their author stated, "The tales are extremely simple and unadorned. They are real conversations of a real child and her mother." Due to popular demand, the series was later (1910) published as a book, *Bible Stories Told to "Toddles."* The engaging conversational style of this book lends itself well as a bedtime read-aloud that allows Jesus to come alive in the Gospels. The study aids include discussion questions to help foster spiritual conversation, Bible excerpts relevant to the presented story, "Growing in Holiness" suggestions for living the Gospel message in our daily lives, and short catechism lessons for both children and adults.

I Talk with God: The Art of Prayer and Meditation for Catholic Children strives to instill in young Catholics a love of prayer and a practical knowledge of the art of meditation. This prayer book contains prayers to pray out loud (vocal prayer) or in the silence of your heart. It shows how you can talk with God, and more importantly, how you can love God. As you progress through this book—from discovering what prayer is to reading and reciting simple prayers to understanding meditation and then to helps for deeper meditation—you will see that prayer and meditation often go together. Meditation is described by the big *Catechism of the Catholic Church* as nothing more than "prayerful reflection" or *holy thinking*. You can use books, devotions, pictures, holy cards, and images (such as the stained glass windows in church) to help you think about holy people, events, and ideas. Learn how to talk with God each day to increase your love for Him and follow more closely His holy will.

Communion with the Saints: A Family Preparation Program for First Communion and Beyond in the Spirit of St. Therese imitates St. Therese of the Child Jesus and her family who studied and prayed for sixty-nine days in anticipation of Therese's First Holy Communion. Modeling this preparation, the *Communion with the Saints* program will help any family find renewed fervor in the reception of the Eucharist. This resource includes a chapter-by-chapter study of the following four books:

- *The Little Flower, The Story of Saint Therese of the Child Jesus*—to provide the foundation of God's love for us and to encourage a desire for holiness
- *The Children of Fatima and Our Lady's Message to the World*—to show the sinfulness of our world and the need to avoid sin
- *The Patron Saint of First Communicants, The Story of Blessed Imelda Lambertini*—to inspire devotion to the Sacrament of Holy Communion
- *The King of the Golden City* by Mother Mary Loyola—to illustrate Jesus' Presence as a source of grace necessary to live a holy life

Each of the sixty-nine days of preparation includes read-aloud selections with enrichment activities, meditational readings, catechism lessons, and plenty of practical application to promote a growth in holiness and sanctity. Weekend suggestions include a list of over thirty-five family projects. The use of *My First Communion Journal* is encouraged with this program.

My First Communion Journal in Imitation of Saint Therese, The Little Flower provides a lasting keepsake of a child's First Holy Communion. This journal has been constructed in imitation of the copybook made for Therese Martin by her older sister Pauline to help Therese prepare for her First Holy Communion. Although this book is not an exact replica of the copybook used by Therese, it does contain many of the same prayers and aspirations she used, the same idea of flowers inspiring virtue, and the same method of recording prayers recited and sacrifices made. It is up to you to decorate and complete this journal, replicating Therese's heroic efforts by raising your mind and heart to Jesus and by humbling yourself with small sacrifices. Learn as well to imitate St. Therese's love and knowledge of Scripture as you meditate on—or even memorize—the biblical passages that are provided for reflection. This journal may be completed in conjunction with the *Communion with the Saints* program or used separately.

My First Communion Journal in Imitation of St. Paul, Putting on the Armor of God was also inspired by St. Therese's copybook and uses the same method of encouraging—and recording—daily prayers and mortifications. However, instead of using flowers to illustrate virtues, this resource uses the battle model St. Paul describes in Ephesians 6:10-17. First communicants are encouraged to arm themselves with virtues and spiritual weapons in order to fight as soldiers of Christ. The scriptural words of Jesus and St. Paul are reflected on frequently to encourage the imitation of the actions and love of Jesus and to inspire a love and knowledge of Holy Scripture. This journal too may be completed in conjunction with the *Communion with the Saints* program or used separately.

The King of the Golden City Study Edition is a new edition of a book that was originally published in 1921. This treasure of a book was written in response to a student's appeal for instructions along with "little stories" to help her prepare for Holy Communion. To fulfill this request, Mother Loyola of the Bar Convent in York, England, wrote a simple story that illustrates Jesus' desire to share an intimate relationship with each one of His children. This new edition contains some updated language but, quite deliberately, does not contain any pictures. Readers, as they progress through this story, will form a mental image of their King, one as unique and personal as their own relationship with Him. The study sections assist with the allegory, connect to the Bible as well as to the catechism, and explore the art of prayer in the spirit of the three Carmelite Doctors of the Church. Although written over ninety years ago for a young child, this book remains a timeless masterpiece of Catholic literature suitable for all ages. (Also available as a study guide only)

The Good Shepherd and His Little Lambs Study Edition is a simply told Catholic tale of four children who meet with their beloved aunt for "First Communion talks." More than a story, it is a First Communion primer that takes the tenets of the catechism and, through naturally-flowing conversations, relates them in the language of little ones to authentic Christian living. As Mrs. Bosch explains, "We might learn the catechism all the way through beautifully, and at the end find ourselves still very stiff and clumsy about loving our Lord. When He comes to us, we don't want to welcome Him into our souls only with answers out of the catechism, do we?" Enriched by appropriate Biblical passages, points of doctrine, and prayers, this story-primer is an enjoyable and effective read-aloud that will prepare the Good Shepherd's little lambs to worthily receive Him in the Holy Eucharist.

A Reconciliation Reader-Retreat: Read-Aloud Lessons, Stories, and Poems for Young Catholics Preparing for Confession provides a basic doctrinal explanation and review of the Sacrament of Reconciliation as well as a Gospel examination of conscience—a seven-day read-aloud formation retreat. To help the lessons come alive and to enable young Catholics to more readily apply these doctrines to their own daily lives, the lessons have been supplemented with pertinent short stories and poems. Each lesson contains reflection questions, a family prayer, and a "Gospel Examination of Conscience" that is formulated according to the dictates of the *Catechism of the Catholic Church*. This reader-retreat will not only enrich and deepen the sacramental experience for each member of your family but it will also provide several tools to help you recommit to leading a virtuous life and to grow together in holiness.

Devotion to St. Joseph: Read-Aloud Stories, Poems, and Prayers for Catholic Children encourages children to love Jesus as St. Joseph did. As Scripture does not record a single word this great saint spoke; we must take our lessons of his life from his actions. In this compilation of stories and poems about our Savior's foster-father from renowned Catholics, children of all ages are encouraged to imitate the virtues the life of St. Joseph reveal to us in his loving dedication to Jesus and Mary. The discussion questions as well as the reflections on the virtues of St. Joseph lead children to apply the lessons of this saint's life to their own while the prayer section promotes a lasting devotion to the great St. Joseph. As St. Teresa of Avila declared, "I wish I could persuade everyone to be devoted to this glorious saint!"

The Month of St. Joseph: Prayers and Practices for Each Day of March in Imitation of the Virtues of St. Joseph was originally published in 1874. This book contains daily meditations on the life and virtues of St. Joseph for adults and high-school students. In addition, each day presents a prayer to St. Joseph, several resolutions, a short ejaculatory prayer, a relevant Scripture verse, and a brief consideration for reflection. The practices for each day are intended to assist the reader in acquiring the habits of prayer and interior recollection so necessary to living in the presence of God. Perfect for Lenten reading, this journey through the life of St. Joseph reveals his love of God and neighbor, humility, quiet action, and spirit of sacrifice. While the Bible tells so little about St. Joseph's life, here we discover the abundant virtues of this silent saint—and are challenged to imitate them.

Alternative Book Reports for Catholic Students contains forty-five book report ideas to encourage critical thinking for ages seven to fourteen. These ideas are intended to provoke a reflection on those themes and topics that support and encourage Catholic living as well as some that may conflict with our Faith. Many report topics require an examination of our personal faith life and prompt us to take lessons from the saints to strengthen our own faith in God. The suggested activities vary from written exercises to creative art projects and include twenty-one topics specifically designed for saint biographies. Other activities can be used within a group or family.

Reading the Saints: Lists of Catholic Books for Children Plus Book Collecting Tips for the Home and School Library (formerly entitled *Saintly Resources*) is a valuable tool for Catholic home educators, classroom teachers, and collectors of Catholic juvenile books. This resource will help you discover living books from such popular out-of-print Catholic juvenile series as Catholic Treasury, Vision Books, and American Background Books as well as current series books for young Catholics. Use this book to find:

- Over 800 Catholic books listed by author, series, reading level, century, and geographical location
- More than 275 authors of saint biographies, historical fiction, and poetry written for Catholic juvenile readers
- Publishers of Catholic children's books, present and past
- Helpful advice for collecting and caring for used books
- Hundreds of age-appropriate, accessible living books to enrich your study of the Catholic Church's rich heritage of saints and notable Catholic historical figures
- Information on how to build and maintain your own library of Catholic juvenile books
- Inspiring quotations about book collecting, reading, and the love of books

The Outlaws of Ravenhurst Study Edition contains a classic story of the persecution of Scottish Catholics that was first written in 1923 and was revised and reprinted in 1950. This 2009 edition of Sr. M. Imelda Wallace's *Outlaws of Ravenhurst* contains the revised story of 1950 plus chapter-by-chapter aids to assist readers in assimilating the book's strong Catholic elements into their own lives. The study section focuses on critical thinking, integration of biblical teachings, and the study of the virtuous life to which Christ calls us as mature Catholics. With its emphasis on virtues (theological and moral plus the gifts and fruits of the Holy Spirit), the spiritual and corporal works of mercy, and the Beatitudes, *Outlaws of Ravenhurst Study Edition* is a fun and effective catechetical tool for Catholics preparing for the Sacrament of Confirmation. (Also available as a study guide only)

The Family that Overtook Christ Study Edition: The Story of the Family of St. Bernard of Clairvaux is an excellent read for young adults who are preparing to receive the Sacrament of Confirmation. In this exciting chronicle of the life of twelfth-century knights, we have an entire family of nine saints who lay before us their individual means of achieving intimate union with Christ. Learn with the Fontaines family how to supernaturalize the natural, develop a God-consciousness, and attain sanctity by being yourself. Perfect for high-school read-aloud (or adult study), this new study edition has over 250 footnotes for increased comprehension and provides discussion/meditation points to promote the art of spiritual conversation. The appendix lists formulas of Catholic doctrine that are essential for confirmands not only to know but also to incorporate into their own spiritual lives.

A Confirmation Reader-Retreat: Read-Aloud Lessons, Stories and Poems for Young Catholics utilizes chapters from two excellent out-of-print Catholic books for children (*I Belong to God, Great Truths in Simple Stories for Children and Lovers of Children* by Lillian Clark; and *Children's Retreats in Preparation for First Confession, First Holy Communion, and Confirmation* by Rev. P.A. Halpin). This book provides a basic doctrinal review of the Sacrament of Confirmation as well as prayer experiences—a nine-day read-aloud retreat/novena. The reprinted material has been supplemented with short stories and poems that provide insights in applying catechetical doctrines to the daily life of young Catholics. Each lesson concludes with "I Talk with God"—a section that encourages readers (of all ages) to deepen their relationship with each of the Three Persons of the Blessed Trinity. Reflection questions promote the habit of spiritual conversation within your family—to encourage family members to discuss holy topics—and to help you grow together in holiness. Additionally, a traditional novena to the Holy Spirit is included.

By Cross and Anchor Study Edition: The Story of Frederic Baraga on Lake Superior relates the exciting, and often miraculous, missionary adventures of the "Snowshoe Priest"—Venerable Frederic Baraga, the first bishop of Michigan's Upper Peninsula. Declared "Venerable" by Pope Benedict XVI on May 10, 2012, this priest came to the United States from Slovenia in 1830 to undertake his mission as a "simple servant of God." For almost forty years, Fr. Frederic Baraga traveled across over 80,000 square miles of wilderness by snowshoe in winter and canoe in summer. In imitation of Christ, Bishop Baraga become poor so that he might bring the riches of the Catholic Faith to the Chippewa and immigrant residents of the beautiful peninsula he served. Although not strictly a biography, this book is a story based on historical facts drawn from Bishop Baraga's own journal and letters—a fascinating, easy-to-read history of Michigan's northern peninsula. While this exciting adventure is intended for youth who are interested in knowing more about this quiet, courageous priest, readers of all ages will be inspired by his life of humility, simplicity, and selfless virtue. This new study edition contains over 130 footnotes, defining less familiar vocabulary words and—gleaned from Venerable Baraga's *Journal* and other primary sources—details regarding the region's people and places. Also included are discussion questions, applicable Scripture passages, pertinent quotations of Venerable Baraga from the text, and—most importantly—a section illustrating how to imitate the various virtues of Venerable Frederic Baraga. Additionally, the complete text of Bishop Baraga's 1853 "Pastoral Letter to the Faithful" has been included with numerous references added in order that we may read this in light of Scripture and the *Compendium of the Catechism of the Catholic Church*. Learn more about the life, ministry, and heroic virtues of Venerable Frederic Baraga, the "Snowshoe Priest."

To Order: Email info@RACEforHeaven.com or place an order at RACEforHeaven.com. Discover, MasterCard, VISA, PayPal, American Express, checks, and money orders are accepted.

www.ingramcontent.com/pod-product-compliance
Lightning Source LLC
Chambersburg PA
CBHW081839170426
43199CB00017B/2782